Summer and Fables

Following the publication of the rehearsal script to coincide with the National Theatre premiere in January 1982, *Summer* is now re-published as a Methuen Modern Play in a completely revised definitive edition which takes account of all the changes made during production.

Summer is set in Eastern Europe in and around a house overlooking the sea. The play centres on an encounter between two women, whose pasts are terribly bound up with the German wartime occupation of the town and nearby islands. Forty years ago, Xenia's family threw dinner parties for the German officers in that very house; Marthe, the family servant, was taken prisoner along with many of the townspeople and condemned to be shot. Only Xenia's intervention saved Marthe's life.

But now, Xenia lives in England and Marthe still lives in the house. Xenia's visit – and the news that Marthe is dying of an incurable disease – provokes a searing reappraisal of the meaning of past events and of the present.

Also included in this volume is a selection of short stories by Edward Bond, *Fables*.

The photograph on the front cover shows Yvonne Bryceland as Marthe, David Yelland as David and Eleanor David as Ann in the National Theatre production. Both this and the photograph of Edward Bond on the back cover are by Chris Davies.

D0165478

Edward Bond

SUMMER

and

FABLES

with

Service

a story

METHUEN · LONDON

Summer first published in Great Britain in 1982 in the Methuen New Theatrescript series by Methuen London Ltd, 11 New Fetter Lane, London EC4P 4EE. Re-issued as a Methuen Paperback and simultaneously as a Hardback in the Methuen Modern Plays series in this re-set and revised edition in 1982.

Summer copyright © 1982 by Edward Bond
Fables copyright © 1982 by Edward Bond
The Dragon, The Boy Who Threw Bread on the Water, The Boy Who Tried to Reform the Thief, The Good Traveller, The Cheat and *The Fly* first published by Calder in *New Writing and Writers 19*.

Service first published in *Fireweed*.

Printed in Great Britain by
Richard Clay (The Chaucer Press) Ltd,
Bungay, Suffolk

ISBN 0 413 49310 5 (Hardback)
ISBN 0 413 50970 2 (Paperback)

Summer

For Hans Werner Henze

Summer

I wanted to show how ordinary people lived
Married gave birth ate had holidays
And died
But clearly ordinary lives are strange
All who live now are survivors of wars and massacres and
   great dangers
We have witnessed the degeneration of our kind more than
   once
We still arm after the strategy of the insane
The starving queue up to die among us
All this is part of our daily life
To ignore it is as fatal as bearing its blows
But I wondered how we could bear it
The body is frail
The voice can be drowned by an engine
The young are taught folly

    Here is a simple story
    Of war and its aftermath
    Which shows that as we live in history
    We cannot learn to bear the unbearable but seek justice
    And praises those who share the earth

To The Audience

Relations between people can't be described without using
   values
But a play is about the nature of values
How can you know its meaning when you need values to
   find it?
Perhaps your values are being questioned
Certainly a play must question or strengthen them
Well, people are on the move and so doors are open
Communication is possible

The artist admits he may be wrong
He hopes he hasn't attracted your attention unnecessarily
He says only that to write the play he used the values by
    which he lives
And that in judging it you use the values by which you live
And show who you are – it is inescapable

Art can't avoid this effrontery
It describes the relations between people and so the
    spectator is judged
At least this makes criticism democratic
But remember: democracy is a more wrathful tyrant than a
    dictator

What Sort of Morality Is That!

Friends or enemies shake hands
Crowds wave at heroes and murderers
Judas kissed
On the Berlin Station platform the mädchen gave a bouquet
To the SS chief who returned from inspecting the eastern
    camps
You can smile and smile
You can kneel in reverence or fear
Yet though it's true a workman spits on his hands
And to clean a child's face a mother will spit on her
    handkerchief
When someone spits at another a spit is a spit
Or is it?

Years after supervising the slaughter
Each morning an unnamed soldier drives to his office
How can we know what he is and so judge what he says and
    does
When he reaches his office?

The dead had a number tattooed on their arm
If we tattooed the soldier with all these numbers
He would be known
But he has too little skin
The numbers would run together
It would take many skins to record his crimes

It is hard for us to know ourselves
But at least we could bear our label so that others know us
And then we will bear the consequence of being ourself
Otherwise in the end
(Which isn't far: history sums up at least twice each
    century)
Others must bear it

Avoid hate as an obsession that clouds judgement
But forgiveness is not yours to give if the dead have paid for
    it
The dead are still unburied
(In this century wherever you turn the spade to bury them
You unearth others)
And then there are the living

You want to forgive the crimes that have not yet been
    committed
What sort of morality is that!

If

If Auschwitz had been in Hampshire
There would have been Englishmen to guard it
To administer records
Marshall transports
Work the gas ovens
And keep silent
The smoke would have drifted over these green hills

It's not that all men are evil or creatures of instinct
We – even our subjective self – are products of history
Of political change
In history two things join
Our will and things beyond our will
We change what we are as a means of controlling those
    things
That is: we create a new culture
We remain human only by changing
Each generation must create its own humanity

Our culture makes us barbarians
It does not allow us to live humanely
We must create a new culture
Or cease to be human
And the smoke will drift over these green hills

Always She Meant Well
(How a character is formed)

Always she meant well
But for some time there had been no need
For there to be rich and poor in her world
It was as if the poor were starved
So that she could bring soup to their door

This led to confusion
The poor disliked poverty and were grateful for handouts
But they resented the lady since in the end
They were asked to be grateful for being poor!

As she gave she saw the resentful smiles
She gave more and became harsh in her kindness
The smiles did not change
She meant well but they treated her so badly!

Her goodness seemed to bring out the worst in them!
Soon being good made her anxious
She turned into a misunderstood lady
Who helped the poor though they were undeserving
And supported everything that repressed them
Because she now knew they could not be trusted
And were a threat to civilization

You'd be surprised
How bitter and angry her goodness made her!
Out of kindness she brought forth reaction
Her world was unjust and had no place for kindness
Kindness became just another act of aggression

Summer was first presented in the Cottesloe Theatre (National Theatre), on 27 January 1982, with the following cast:

DAVID	David Yelland
XENIA	Anna Massey
ANN	Eleanor David
MARTHE	Yvonne Bryceland
GERMAN	David Ryall

Directed by Edward Bond
Designed by Hayden Griffin
Lighting by Rory Dempster
Sound by Rick Clarke

Scenes
1. House. Night.
2. House. Morning.
3. House. Afternoon.
4. Island. Late afternoon.
5. House. Night.
6. House. Morning.
7. House. Late morning.

In the first production there was an interval after Scene 5.

The present.
Eastern Europe.

The terrace of a cliff house facing the sea.
Down right a door leads downstairs to the street.
Up right a door leads upstairs to other parts of the house.
In the wall at the back, left, a door leads to a room.
Left, railings face the sea.

ONE

The house. Night.
DAVID comes in with XENIA and ANN. He carries cases.
XENIA and ANN carry hand luggage.

DAVID: You're in your old room. I'm sorry I couldn't meet you at the airport.

XENIA: It doesn't matter.

DAVID (*smiles*): I'd swapped with a colleague to have the morning off.

XENIA: It wasn't your fault our plane was late. We sat at Heathrow all day.

DAVID: I'll take these things up and fetch the rest from below.

ANN: I'll help you.

DAVID: No no, I can manage. You must be tired.

> *DAVID goes.*

XENIA (*calling after him*): Where's Marthe?

ANN (*glances round*): Nothing's changed.

XENIA: You don't know it as well as I do. That hideous new hotel. A dreadful holiday camp stood on end. I shouldn't complain. People must have holidays. I'll be all right tomorrow. Waiting at airports always depresses me. It's so inefficient. At least they've left the sea where it was. Thank God you don't see the hotel from here. You'll see it from below.

> *DAVID comes in with two cases. He nods at a case already there.*

DAVID: I'll come back for that.

XENIA: Where's your mother?

DAVID: Resting.

XENIA: I suppose your new hotel has a discotheque?

DAVID: Wednesdays and Saturdays.

> DAVID *goes upstairs.* XENIA *follows him out. She takes her hand luggage.* ANN *is alone. She goes to the railing and looks at the sea.* DAVID *comes back.*

DAVID (*points to the case*): Shall I put that in your room?

ANN: Yes.

DAVID: I'm glad you're back.

ANN: Thank you.

DAVID: Are you tired?

ANN: A little.

DAVID: I have to work in the morning. I have the afternoon off. I'll take you swimming.

ANN: Thank you.

DAVID: I've arranged to have most of my time off while you're here. I have to go in some mornings to see a sick child.

XENIA (*off, calls*): Ann.

ANN (*calls*): Coming. (*To* DAVID:) You mustn't inconvenience your colleagues because of me.

DAVID: It's part of my holidays.

> ANN *goes.* DAVID *is alone. He taps on the rear door.*

(*Low:*) She's gone upstairs.

> DAVID *sits. He stretches his legs in front of him and broods. After a few moments the door opens and* MARTHE *comes out.*

MARTHE: When I hear her voice it's as if I'm back in the past.

DAVID: Why let her come?

MARTHE: I can't stop her. Anyone can book the guest rooms.

DAVID: Say they're already booked.

MARTHE: Don't be a child. I don't mind her.

DAVID: She upsets you. Let me send her away.

MARTHE: It would be cruel to do it now. Let things go on as before.

DAVID: As you please. But don't see her tonight. That can wait till the morning.

MARTHE: Yes, that would be best.

ANN *comes in.*

ANN: Hello.

MARTHE: My dear. (*She kisses* ANN.) Was it a dreadful journey?

ANN: The plane took off late. We had to wait at the airport. We couldn't leave because our flight could have been called at any time.

XENIA (*off, calls*): Ann darling.

ANN: Excuse me. (*Calls:*) Yes?

XENIA (*off, calls*): Bring my keys. I want to undo my cases.

ANN (*calls*): I haven't got them.

XENIA (*off, calls*): I gave them to you when we left the house.

ANN (*calls*): They're in your handbag.

XENIA (*off, calls*): Oh no, you've left them behind. It's too much.

ANN (*calls*): Look in your handbag.

MARTHE (*moving towards her room*): Will you want anything to eat?

ANN: No, we've been eating all day.

MARTHE: You look well.

ANN: Thank you.

MARTHE: A little pale. You'll soon catch the sun. Till the morning. We'll breakfast together.

MARTHE *goes into her room and shuts the door.*

DAVID: Has she lost her keys?

ANN: I don't know. Anyway a lot of her things are in my cases.

DAVID: How's your father?

ANN: Always the same. He's on a diet. He's been on it for years. He enjoys having the house to himself while we're away.

DAVID: I thought you were a happy family.

ANN: We are. We never quarrel. I meant it must be nice when there's no one to bump into.

DAVID: Shall I come to your room tonight?

ANN: No, if you don't mind. The journey's tired me.

DAVID: It's all right. You'll feel better after you've slept. Would your mother like a drink?

ANN: I'll ask when I go up.

DAVID: Is anything wrong?

ANN: Oh, please. I've been travelling with strangers all day. Surely it's natural for me to want to be quiet? It doesn't mean I'm ill, does it? Why must you – intrude all the time?

DAVID: You've grown very beautiful this year.

XENIA *comes in.*

XENIA: I was in the hallway at the foot of the stairs. Just before we left the house. Daddy had brought the car to the front. I gave them to you to mind and went back to make sure Timmy was shut in the kitchen. You remember?

ANN: No.

XENIA: It's too much. On top of everything. Sometimes one can't rely on you at all. Have you looked for them?

ANN: I haven't got them.

XENIA: Give me your bag. (*She looks in* ANN'*s travelling bag. She finds keys.*) These are yours.

ANN: Yes.

XENIA: How absurd. I'll have to break the locks. The three cases will be ruined. Shops won't replace locks on cases anymore. David, have you got any case keys?

DAVID: Yes, in my room.

XENIA: Did you buy your cases in the West?

DAVID: No.

XENIA: Then your keys won't fit my locks. Please bring me a hammer and a robust screwdriver.

DAVID: No. It's silly to break them. I'll get some keys for you to try in the morning. Ann or my mother will lend you what you need till then.

XENIA: I like to feel at home in this house – unpack my things and hang them in their place. Now there's all this muddle. I might as well be in a hotel.

DAVID: You've had a bad day.

XENIA: Well, at least Ann brought her own keys. We must be grateful she didn't leave them behind with mine. It will do me good to put up with the inconvenience. I'm not a good traveller. I don't know why Ann travels with me. If we had the same luggage your keys would have fitted mine. Have you looked in your pockets?

ANN: You didn't give me your keys.

XENIA: Well, if you did put them in your pocket they'll have dropped out in the plane or the airport, so I hope you didn't.

DAVID: Would you like a drink?

XENIA: I'm surprised they didn't build the hotel on one of the islands. Yes, I know the islands are a national monument. That wouldn't stop them. Can you still bathe from these rocks?

DAVID: Why not?

XENIA: Doesn't the hotel litter float by?

DAVID: The odd ice cream carton.

XENIA: I shall telephone Daddy in the morning and ask him

to look for my keys on the hall table. I hope he doesn't find them before I telephone.

DAVID: A military man would survive the shock.

XENIA: It isn't a question of shock. It would distress him to know I had been unable to open my cases after a tiring journey. That's why I want to reassure him I'm not upset. It's a question of two people caring for one another.

ANN: I don't see the point of knowing they're on the hall table.

XENIA: If I know they're there I won't spend the whole of the holiday worrying about them. Are the telephones working?

DAVID: Yes.

XENIA: They didn't two years ago.

DAVID: That was after the hurricane.

XENIA: So it was. Where's Marthe?

DAVID: In her room.

XENIA: Is she unwell?

DAVID: She lives down here now.

XENIA: Why?

DAVID: To be next to the terrace. She sits there during the day.

XENIA:: What's the matter? She's ill.

DAVID: Yes.

XENIA: Seriously? I must go to her.

DAVID: You'll see her in the morning. She needs rest.

XENIA: But what's the matter with her? Why didn't you tell me before?

DAVID: I didn't have a chance.

XENIA: Nonsense. You could have told me down in the street.

DAVID: She has a reticulosis.

XENIA: What's that? Please don't confuse me with medical jargon.

DAVID: It's a disease of the lymphatic glands.

XENIA: Is it serious?

DAVID: Yes, it's terminal.

XENIA: But she'll get better?

DAVID: No.

XENIA: You think she . . .?

DAVID: Yes.

XENIA: David what are you telling me? Surely there's a cure? (*Panic whisper*:) Dear god, can she hear us? Really David I think you might have told me sooner. That ridiculous fuss about my keys.

DAVID: It doesn't matter. Please don't upset yourself.

XENIA: Of course I'm upset. It's a terrible shock.

DAVID: Yes.

XENIA: Is there no cure?

DAVID: No.

XENIA: Oh god. Is she in pain? Our holiday is off. You should have written and told me.

DAVID: She wouldn't let me write. You'd have come any-way.

XENIA: Certainly, to nurse her – or help in some other way. You must tell me what to do.

DAVID: Don't strain her. Just behave as you normally would.

XENIA: Of course, of course. How long will it take? You can't possibly know. Tell me the worst so I'm prepared. Is she in pain? Can she walk?

DAVID: You won't see much change so far. She has no pain. We've known for six weeks she was dying. I don't know how much longer she'll live. It doesn't shock her now. She knows it's true.

XENIA: Are you treating her?

DAVID: Yes.

XENIA: David, I'm so sorry.

DAVID: Yes, it's very sad.

XENIA: She's lucky to have you. You will tell me what I can do? Nursing, washing, anything.

DAVID: Thank you, but there is nothing.

XENIA: And you, if we can help you in any way. It's terrible for you. You are so close. We mustn't stay here gossiping. She must have rest and quiet.

DAVID: You've forgotten what else I said. Please behave as you normally would. Otherwise you'll frighten her and aggravate her condition.

XENIA: Yes, of course. David, goodnight. Ann, come with me.

DAVID: Goodnight.

> XENIA *goes.* ANN *looks at* DAVID *and then follows her mother out. He sits hunched in the chair and empties his mind.*

TWO

The house. Morning.
MARTHE *sits in her chair up left.*
XENIA *comes in.*

XENIA: Marthe.

MARTHE: Hello. How are you? (XENIA *kisses her.*)

XENIA: Oughtn't you to lie down? I'm surprised David lets you sit out here.

MARTHE: Did you sleep well?

XENIA: Would you expect me to? I was so tired when I arrived. We'd spent all day at Heathrow. After David told me you were ill I hardly slept at all. He seems very pessimistic about this lymphatic-thing. Sometimes doctors almost sound proud of the diseases they're treating. They like to look on the dark side so that they can claim a miracle cure. It's good for their reputation even if it's bad for their patients. Let me get you a shawl.

MARTHE: I'd be far too hot.

XENIA: My mother moved into that room whenever she was ill.

MARTHE: So she did. I'd forgotten.

XENIA: Fortunately I can stay on this year till you're better. Ann will look after the boutique. It's time she learned to stand on her own feet. I can keep in touch by telephone. I'll have to go back for the spring buy but that won't –

MARTHE: I can't disrupt your life like that.

XENIA: Well, I've offered. I hope you change your mind.

MARTHE: Thank you. We'll see.

XENIA: What d'you do all day?

MARTHE: I can still do a little work. Mostly I sit and look at the sea.

XENIA: I don't like to see you resigned like this. You seem to have given in. You're still young, your life is worth saving. How can you be sure nothing can be done? Because David's your son I suppose you find it hard to believe he's wrong. Doctors do make mistakes – more than the rest of us. Who made the diagnosis? Have you taken a second opinion? Has David discussed your treatment with a specialist?

MARTHE: Everything was done as it should be.

XENIA: Modern medicine moves so fast. They do things now that would have been miracles a few years ago. If you'd telephoned I'd have brought drugs from England. I don't know how up-to-date David's clinic is or if they have any equipment. He'd be cross if I asked.

MARTHE: He does all that can be done for me. Which isn't hard – there's very little. Did you find your keys?

XENIA: I knew my shouting woke you last night.

MARTHE: I wasn't asleep.

XENIA: David said he would get me some keys this morning. O let's not worry about the wretched things. Do you have pain?

MARTHE: No. I get tired, but that's more mental than physical. The strain.

XENIA: Come to England. David has money. And Bertie and I would help. A gift – or a loan if you wished. You could go to a private clinic for a check-up. Surely David wouldn't stop you. I've seen other people in your situation. You'll leave it and make up your mind when it's late. Then they'd have to bring you in a wheelchair. Another excuse for them to do nothing: the journey would be too tiring.

MARTHE: David says nothing can be done.

XENIA: He can't know that. I've been told not to tire you so I'll be careful. But at least I can ask you to take a fresh look at yourself. That can't do any harm! Fight. Don't sit in a chair and wait. I'm glad I didn't know you were ill before I came. I can see what's happening with a fresh mind. You're all so apathetic. You've resigned yourself as if you were meeting fate. It's not like you. A doctor's word isn't law.

MARTHE: I don't want to die.

XENIA: At least you can still talk sense. I'm sorry, but you're irresponsible. It's criminal to stay here. If you went you'd have a chance.

ANN *comes in.*

ANN (*showing two large hoops of keys*): Look. (*She kisses* XENIA.)

XENIA (*half-attention*): Good heavens, there must be hundreds.

ANN (*kisses* MARTHE): Hello. I borrowed them from the hotel.

XENIA: Obviously they hadn't heard of your way with keys.

ANN: David came with me. I'll go and try them. Cross your fingers.

XENIA: Don't force the locks.

ANN *goes.*

All this fuss. If they're broken they're broken. I'll get some cheap ones in town to last till I get home. You can have the old ones. Perhaps you can still get locks fitted here. If not they'll be useful for something. She slept with David last year. Obviously he'll be thinking about other things now. Has he a steady girl? Most young doctors seem to have several unsteady ones. Ann would never live here.

MARTHE: Has she said?

XENIA: O she knows too much about the past. It would be a terrible wrong to a child to force it to fight its parents' battles. We do them enough harm without that. I've never forced my views on her. I've simply told her the truth. Children have a right to know the world they're in. I showed her the spot that used to be the library where her grandfather was arrested. I showed her the walls of the prison where he died. I showed her where his pictures hung in this house. You can still see the marks if you know where to look. Even when they paint the walls they come through again in a few months. She knows the history of every stone in this house.

MARTHE: Why do you come here every year? There are other places where you could find the sun. You're married, you have money, your own shop. You have a new life.

XENIA: It's natural to want to come back to the place where you were born. Even if it's another world. This house was my home for twenty years. I have friends who've lived on in the town. I like to speak my own language.

MARTHE: Wipe our dust from your feet. That's good advice. This isn't your home anymore. You're a stranger here. Some of the flats have changed hands eight or nine times since you left. Most of the people in them have never heard your family name.

XENIA: The trees in the garden are the same. The lizards must be distant offspring of the ones who were my pets when I was a child. It's the same sea even if it's dirtier. There are still two islands. Some of the cacti I planted on my visits have survived. I come to water them. People put out their cigarette butts in the soil. Lean from the side of their canvas chairs and grind out their cigarettes in it. That's such an ugly thing to do. It desecrates the earth. There's nothing you can say.

ANN *comes in.*

ANN: The third one. I've hung your things in the wardrobe.
XENIA: Bless you. Make a note of the key numbers. I'll telephone Daddy this evening and ask him to send duplicates. We must hope the post delivers them before we go. Don't lose those before you get them back to the hotel.
ANN: Marthe would you like us to go away?
MARTHE: No. Unless staying depresses you.
ANN: It's just that there's nothing we can do to help.
MARTHE: That's not true. Don't be sorry for me. As David can look after me I can stay here to die. I've lived on the sea since I was a child. I'd be unhappy if it was taken away now. David says he can make sure I'll feel no pain.
ANN: What is it like to be told?
XENIA (*reproof*): Ann.
MARTHE: At first I was sick. Out of fear I suppose. Once when people knew they were dying they prayed and confessed and worried like a dog that had lost its bone. They wasted the little time they had left trying to get a promise they would live for ever. Ridiculous. They could never even know the promise hadn't been given. Death is the most certain of all things yet it's the thing people try to create the most doubt about. When you die you're dead. You don't wake up. There's nothing. This is my last chance of happiness. We all share our lives. If your lives go on in their normal way, so will mine for a little longer. If they don't, I've already started to die. I don't want to do

that till I have to. So let's go on as we did before. That's
how you can help me.

XENIA: I can't. David says you're dying. That changes
everything. I don't know what to do yet – or what to think.

MARTHE: You'll get used to it.

XENIA: You've had six weeks. I'll need more than one day.

ANN: David's taking me out in his boat this afternoon. We'll
go for miles and swim in the deep sea. Far out, so that the
coast keeps bobbing below the waves. I know you like it
there. Come with us.

XENIA: I'd feel as if I were splashing in a puddle.

DAVID *comes in.*

DAVID: Did they fit?

ANN: Yes.

XENIA: Thank you David.

DAVID: Well that problem's solved. I'll borrow them again
for you when you leave. Now you can forget all about it and
enjoy your holiday. You're quiet. Have you rowed?

XENIA: You are supposed to be at work.

DAVID: My mother has reticulosis. To be precise a lymphosarcome. The diagnosis is certain but details of the
prognosis are not. My mother might live for only a few
months from the onset of her illness. A number of new
treatments are available here and abroad. A typical
example is cis-Platinum. It's given in a drip and causes the
patient to vomit for several days. It doesn't appreciably
prolong life. I treat my mother with chlorambucil. Doctors
have used it for twenty years. Lymphocytes are white
blood cells. There's another sort of white blood cell, the
polymorphonuclear neutrophils. In lymphosarcome the
number of lymphocytes increases greatly, from the normal
one to two thousand per cubic millimetre to fifty thousand
or even a hundred thousand. As it were, they take over.
When such a thing happens the cells circulating in the

peripheral blood are no longer mature lymphocytes but immature ones – or even worse, their precursors the lymphoblasts. There's a rush to destruction, as if a nation losing a war had started to put its children into uniform. Then the ravages of death begin. To reduce my mother's WCC – white cell count – I give her each day six milligrammes of chlorambucil. Her total WCC should be between five thousand and fifteen thousand per cubic millimetre. Last week it was twelve thousand five hundred. Now its eleven thousand. Unfortunately chlorambucil also attacks the other white cells, the polymorphonuclear neutrophils, and these are our main protection against infection. That is to say the treatment attacks the body's defences. Yet we must treat. So there is no escape. If necessary death becomes, as it were, an adverse side-effect of the cure. You will have wondered about the manner of my mother's death. Normally cancer patients progressively weaken and waste away. In time they are bedridden. At the end there is coma sometimes complicated with pneumonia. With the reticuloses there is terminally a tendency to exsanguinate. For example from the upper respiratory tract. A nosebleed. As to hope, we might hope that my mother dies sooner and

ANN *leaves the room.*

so more quickly. She has two chances of this: by coronary thrombosis or pulmonary embolism. Both are on her cards. In coronary thrombosis a coronary artery supplying heart muscle is blocked and the portion of heart muscle normally supplied with blood by that artery dies. If a main coronary artery and consequently a large amount of heart muscle is involved the heart stops immediately. There is collapse, a few stertorous respirations – a sound, we said as students, as of feet struggling to free themselves from quicksand – and then death. My mother is sixty-five. At her age segments of coronary arteries will have been narrowed by plaques of atheroma. A tiny haemorrhage in the depths of such plaque would cause it to swell and occlude the artery. Coronary thrombosis follows. The other possible alternative is pulmonary embolism. In pulmonary embolism a clot or thrombus forms in a vein, breaks loose – after which it's known as an embolus – and begins its long floating journey to the stage right atrium of the heart. A few seconds later it blocks a pulmonary artery. If the clot is gross enough death is virtually instantaneous. Marthe's mobility is reduced and she's a bit dehydrated. Together these factors favour the formation of a clot in a leg or the pelvis. This dvt – deep vein thrombosis – may precede pulmonary embolism by hours or days. It announces itself by a swelling of the calf and foot – if a calf vein is involved – or the whole leg if it occurs in a pelvic, iliofemoral vein. As with coronary thrombosis, death is immediate. If my mother were to die in one of these two ways she would to that extent be fortunate. The body

ANN *comes back with a glass of water.*

has not yet evolved means of terminating its life efficiently on all occasions when it's desirable from the patient's point of view for it to do so.

ANN *gives* XENIA *the glass.*

XENIA (*to* ANN): Thank you. (*To* DAVID:) How interesting. (*She drinks.*)

Off, a drunk sings.

DAVID: A drunk.
XENIA: From the hotel?
DAVID: Clambering over the rocks. So early. On all fours. Like Father Neptune. Last June one was knocked down in front of the hotel. All fours met four wheels.

XENIA: Ann told me you've invited us to swim with you this afternoon. Thank you, I look forward to it. Excuse me. My cases are open and I can change my clothes.

> XENIA *goes.* ANN *sits hunched on the floor by the back wall.*

MARTHE: That wasn't necessary.

DAVID: It was necessary for you not her. She will tempt you, Marthe. Don't fall. You are going to die. If I hadn't told you you could pretend. But you know. As long as you are alive you must choose how to live – even though the end's inevitable. You must agree to die. Otherwise you can't die in peace. The time will come when you can't fool yourself. But you won't be prepared. When that happens to someone they die in bitterness. I've seen it. I don't want you to die like that.

> DAVID *goes left, leans on the railings and watches the sea.*

MARTHE: Bitterness? I'll be glad to die. I welcome it. But why must I wait? This isn't my body anymore. Some horrible bundle I carry round. It's coming undone. God knows what will fall out. (*Goes to* DAVID.) Give me something, David. Don't make me suffer this. David. David. Let me kill myself. My nose is bleeding.

DAVID (*evenly, without turning round*): That woman's undone everything.

MARTHE: Why is my son cruel?

DAVID (*as before*): When Priam came to Achilles and asked for his murdered son's body Achilles said 'That is the fate gods give wretched men to suffer while they are free from care'.

MARTHE (*goes to* ANN *and shows her the blood on her face*): Ann, ask him for me. Perhaps he'll do it for you.

> ANN *edges away along the wall.*

DAVID (*as before*): I must go to the garage to buy petrol for
the boat. Don't come. There'll be a queue of tourists.
The sun and the engines make it as smelly and hot as a
furnace.

MARTHE: Shall I wait till you all die? It won't be long before
you set fire to yourselves. Your generation will have no
memorial. The sound of a whirlwind, the name of a skull:
Hiroshima, Nagasaki. People turned into shadows on their
doorsteps. Human negatives. The dead living.

DAVID: We'll take a picnic on the boat.

MARTHE (*to herself*): Yak. Human rubbish overflowing from
dustbins. Such stench. Dogs mawling it in the gutter. Ha,
cry for that!

ANN: I'm not coming.

DAVID (*as before*): We'll leave in an hour. We come back
when it's dark. You meet the fishing boats going out and
see the men working in the lamp-light on the decks. It
would be better if mother took her tablet at the same time
each day. I can't always get away from the clinic when I
want. You can take charge of her. You'll have to watch her
to see she takes them.

ANN *goes.* DAVID *turns, goes to* MARTHE *and offers her
tissues.*

MARTHE: I managed on my own.

DAVID *tries to help her.*

Don't touch me. I don't need that help.

DAVID *goes.* MARTHE *goes into her room and shuts the
door.*

THREE

The house. Afternoon.
MARTHE *sleeps in her chair.* ANN *reads a book.*
DAVID *comes in.*

DAVID (*quietly, to* MARTHE): I'm off to the clinic.

ANN: She's sleeping.

DAVID: Will you be all right on your own?

ANN: I told you I like to be alone sometimes.

DAVID: Yes. I suppose you're busy at home.

ANN: I suppose so. Work, concerts, cinemas. We have a crowd of friends. Daddy brings officers home from his regiment for mother to entertain. Her cooking is famous. In England it's foreign.

DAVID: Why won't you sleep with me any more?

ANN: What can it lead to? I have to go home soon.

DAVID: We were happy last year. When you left you meant to sleep with me. Why've you changed?

ANN: Last year I was a child.

DAVID: Do you have a man friend in England?

ANN: Yes.

DAVID: Do you sleep with him?

ANN: Yes.

DAVID: Is that why you won't sleep with me?

ANN: No.

DAVID: Will you marry this man?

ANN: I don't know.

DAVID: Has he asked you?

ANN: No.

DAVID: What's his name?

ANN: David there's no point in these questions.

DAVID: Sleep with me tonight.

ANN: No.

VOICE (*off, calls*): Ivan.

DAVID: Why not? Is it because mother's dying? Many towns have natal wards and hospices for the dying in the same grounds. Before you knew my mother was dying did you mean to sleep with me?

ANN: No. I made up my mind on the plane.

DAVID: At least the decision was late.

MARTHE (*wakes startled*): David. (*He goes to her.*) What's the time?

DAVID: Twenty past two. I'm late for the clinic. Are you all right?

MARTHE: Yes.

DAVID (*kisses* MARTHE): Goodbye.

MARTHE: Goodbye.

DAVID *goes.*

MARTHE: Your dress is pretty.

ANN: Mother's boutique. She has good taste.

MARTHE: Is she still in town?

ANN: Yes. She had lunch with a friend.

MARTHE: David looked forward to seeing you. He talked about you a lot – till the last few weeks. Yesterday I remembered something that happened when he was a child. I think of these things because I sit in my chair all day. David can't leave here, Ann. He wouldn't be happy away from the clinic. Would you live here?

ANN: He hasn't asked me. If he did I'd say no. This is mother's house – I know we've been turned out. But that's still how I think of it.

MARTHE: You needn't live in this house.

ANN: I feel as if she was born in the middle ages. What was she like when she was my age?

MARTHE: Very kind. All her family were. They owned half the town. That isn't a figure of speech. Factories, a bank, the local paper, the farms in the hills. Your grandparents were almost royalty. They expected to be bowed at in the streets.

ANN: Were they hated?

MARTHE: Sometimes. They were also loved and respected, which was worse.

ANN: Why?

MARTHE: Some people loved them for what they were, others for what they thought they were. But it didn't matter what they were.

ANN: Why?

MARTHE: When you have so much power you might as well be nobody. Necessity takes over. Factories and banks aren't run by kindness. They run on their own laws. The owners and owned must both obey them. The kindness of one person to another can't change that. If it could the world would be a better place. After all, we all mean well. What decides our lives isn't what the owners are like. They must never be the chosen few – even if they're the best. Your family made the people who loved and respected them confuse kindness with justice. That is corrupting. You can live without kindness, you can't live without justice – or fighting to get it. If you try to you're mad. You don't understand yourself or the world. And then nothing works. You and everyone else suffer the consequences of your madness. Whole generations bleed for it. The state of injustice is always a state of madness.

ANN: You're severe.

MARTHE: Some things require such severity.

> XENIA *comes in.*

XENIA: How are you?

MARTHE: Fine.

ANN: Did you enjoy your visit?

> XENIA *goes out. Almost immediately she returns with a chair and a bottle.*

XENIA: Look, brandy from the duty free shop. Not local fire water. I've already had a tot. Are you allowed to drink some?

MARTHE: Yes please.

XENIA: You're sure? I don't want to be arraigned by the medical authorities.

ANN: I'll get some glasses.

ANN *goes.* XENIA *sits.*

XENIA: My visit wore me out. I sat and listened to three hours of complaints. What can I do? I'm helpless. The neighbours' children are noisy. I shouted at them. They ran away laughing. After fifteen minutes they came back and were even noisier. She has no friends. No one calls. All the people she knew are dead or abroad. Every morning she gets up and brushes her hair into that bun she's worn for fifty years – and it's been grey for twenty.

ANN *comes back with three glasses.*

Then she sits in a chair till the light in its mercy fades and she can creep across her room to bed. You serve. (ANN *pours.*) It upset me. To go on living after the world's been taken away from you. (ANN *gives her a glass.*) Thank you. Cheers. (*She drinks.*) A disgraceful neglect of an old woman.

MARTHE: I'll ask David to call on her.

XENIA: She doesn't need a doctor. She's as tough as a horse or she wouldn't have survived. She needs companionship.

MARTHE: I know. I used to call on her. It became too tiring. She hates so many things. She's thrown her life away.

XENIA: O, I did some shopping. (*From a bag.*) There.

MARTHE *unwraps the parcel.*

MARTHE: What is it?

XENIA: A waiter's crumb brush.

MARTHE: For me?

XENIA: The birds. You throw them your crumbs. Now you can do it in comfort and not waste any. I hope they sing louder. My grandmother gave them as Christmas presents.

ANN: Where did you get it?

XENIA: The old ironmongers. They had a box of them in the back of the storeroom. If you make a fuss they'll find anything. (*She sips.*) This is good. When I was a girl we went to the islands almost every day in the summer. Often we camped there. Mother and father would bring their friends for the day. There was always some young man who could play the mandolin. The women sat under silk sunshades and the men rolled up their trouser-legs and stood in the shallows to fish. I expected an old Chinaman to come out of a cave and kneel to pray or draw a map of the sky in the sand. At night we dived from the rocks and floated in the sea and looked at the stars. I'm sorry. Seeing the old woman upset me. She was my father's friend. She came here to our dinners. After the grown-ups had eaten they sat out here on the terrace. If I was a good child I was allowed to sit with them. The family and guests talked quietly as if they were in awe of the moon, it was so high. On this terrace. And down in the garden. It was a garden then. Often a breeze came off the sea and blew the scents of the flowers and shrubs over us. I sat in my father's lap and listened to his heart and the racing of his watch. He bought his cigars in Paris. Then the farmers sang in the hills. I expect my father paid for their songs. We listened in silence. The farmers worked hard and yet they created that beauty. I fell asleep on my father's lap and woke in my bed. In those days my happiness frightened me – it was so great I thought I would die of it. Long ago. I didn't know that men who sang so beautifully could hate so deeply. I still don't believe it. That's how we lived till the fanatics came. Then the crowds cheered and waved and marched as if the town had been taken over by a circus. And after them came the war. Shells. Sea mines. Foreign uniforms. The ugly little huts on the islands. People hounded and tortured and shot. And when the war was over they threw down the gods and goddesses from the terraces. Zeus, Hera and Aphrodite lay on the rocks with no arms or heads. Our fault. It has all gone. We were foolish. It will never be given back. I hope those who have it are happy. What's the use of saying all this?

ANN: More?

XENIA: A drop. (ANN *pours*.) Thank you.

MARTHE: I want to tell Ann something.

XENIA: O dear, now I've upset Marthe. How silly of me to rake up the past. How stupid.

MARTHE: You know that once I was going to be shot.

ANN: Shot? No! By us?

MARTHE: Haven't you told her?

XENIA (*shrugs*): There seemed no point. (*She sips*.) This is good.

MARTHE: It was the Germans. A German soldier on a motor-bike was shot at. The motor-bike crashed and both the driver and an officer in the sidecar were killed. The Germans took hostages. Two hundred for the officer and a hundred for the driver. In those days when you saw Germans you hid or hurried away. I was trapped in a sidestreet and taken to the islands.

ANN: These islands?

MARTHE: Yes. Your family still owned them then.

XENIA: It was terrible. The Germans commandeered them for a concentration camp. They insisted on paying rent.

MARTHE: Your mother persuaded the German commandant to let me go.

ANN: You saved Marthe's life! Why have you never told me?

XENIA: What was there to tell? We all helped each other under the occupation. I wanted to save them all but I could

only ask for Marthe: she was our servant. The commandant probably thought that if his soldiers shot her it would
make conversation awkward the next time he came to
dinner. He shot the others. We were used to shooting by
then. They shot people every day on the islands. For
months on end. You could hear it on this terrace. The
irony was that father passed information to the partisans
through Marthe. That's why we had the Germans to dine.
They trusted us and we overheard many things that helped
the partisans. You see what a brave grandfather you had. If
the Germans had found out they'd have shot him and his
family. Not that it helped him after the war.

MARTHE: We were shut in a hut for a day and a half. The
barred window had been boarded with planks. Most of us
sat on a wooden bench that ran round the inside of the hut.
There wasn't room on it for everyone. Some sat on the floor
in the middle. We were all women. The men and children
were in other huts.

ANN: Children?

MARTHE: The Germans began to shoot the men. We heard
bursts of firing. I don't know why we didn't go mad.
People seem to be able to bear almost anything. A few
prayed. Some cried. Others cursed. No one turned to the
wall. We looked at each other. Of course I'd known that I
might be shot. But I didn't know how to die. What you did
at the end.

XENIA: That's enough. (*She sips.*)

MARTHE (*she seems to forget the others*): When a German was
shot everything was taken. Papers, uniform, boots,
weapons – everything that could be used. Once – after I'd
been released – I found a wallet on one of them. Inside
there was a photograph of his father and mother. Then one
of his girl. And at the back two of the war. One of these
showed six or seven naked women standing in a group in a
field. The print was blurred. Wartime chemicals. You

couldn't see where they were. There were some trees in the distance and a dark shape that might have been a barn. At one side a grey figure pointed a rifle at them. Very neat and trim. I think his boots were polished. A toy soldier. He must have had other soldiers with him but you couldn't see them. The other photograph also showed women. Two neighbours or a mother and daughter. They were bundled up in clothes and their heads were hidden in scarves. They turned away so that their heads were in shadow. The place was misty or perhaps the film was bad. Wartime quality. The little hill under their feet looked like a cloud. There were no soldiers in this picture. Nothing to show the women were going to be shot. But I knew they were. Immediately. From the gesture of their head and shoulders. It was the gesture of the first photograph. They huddled together and turned away as if it had started to rain. That was how you died. Simply. As if you walked out of life. (*Turns to others.*) I knew by sight some of the women with me in the hut. I'd seen them in town. One woman began to tell us about her life. She'd married an elderly farmer. Her son had been killed in the war. She'd come down to town to sell his clothes and been rounded up. We took turns to say who we were and how we'd lived. We gave our names to pass on if any of us survived. It was as if we were in a schoolroom and were going to die. There was an old woman beside me on the bench. She was so doubled over that if she died facing the soldiers the bullets went in her back. She'd lost everything – her family and her room. When I told them the name of the woman I worked for she said 'If I could live to spit in her face' and spat in the dirt. Later a soldier came in. Most of the women ran to the other end of the hut and wailed. The soldier shouted my name over the noise. I followed him out. While he chained the door he turned to grin at me. He made the thumbs up sign as if I'd won a lottery. He led me along the side of the hut.

You were standing beside an officer. You held the strap of your patent leather handbag in both hands. The soldier saluted. You nodded.

XENIA (*defensively*): To identify you.

MARTHE: The officer clicked and saluted you. I followed you to the landing place and onto the military boat.

XENIA (*confused*): It was windy and choppy. We didn't say anything. If you'd thanked me I'd have laughed.

MARTHE: I spent the next day in my room. I heard the shooting from there. Two hours. I wondered what batch I'd have been in. Several times I thought it was over but it started again.

XENIA: After the war the guards on the island were changed. My father was arrested as an exploiter. Perhaps they put him in Marthe's hut. He was sentenced to ten years hard labour. He escaped by dying in two. My mother had already died during the war. When father was arrested friends took me in. I was smuggled out of the country in an army lorry. That's how I met your father. (*She sips.*) Some of those who arrested him were among those he'd passed information to. What happened as they left the house became a legend in our family. A servant opened the door and my father said 'Thank you'. One of his captors said 'Let him learn to open doors' and another said 'His door will be locked'. They led him away through the garden. There should have been fruit on the trees. A crowd had picked it early. They were too hungry to notice they ate sour fruit. (*She sips.*) I can't understand why you punished him. I understand why you took his house, money, clothes, cattle, land, books, pictures, umbrella – but why punish him? He was an old man who wasn't used to manual work. It was a sentence of death. He had faults. A bad temper. He once hit my mother. But he didn't choose the bed he was born in. He behaved as they all did in his position. Someone must run the world. If you do it better, fine. But why punish him? Nothing was too petty for his trial. Each time he swore at a taxi driver or dismissed someone for bad time-keeping. It was all remembered. They forgave him nothing. Even you gave evidence against him.

MARTHE: I described how he lived. The parties and gambling. Many in the court had starved. It was dangerous to live in your father's world.

ANN: Don't quarrel. Let me think about what you've both told me.

XENIA: Yes, think. And learn what people do in this world. Once those islands were one piece of rock. Then the sea tore them in two. I've seen men and women who could have torn them apart with their bare hands their hatred was so great. How can you sit and look at them all day?

MARTHE: I've lived a second life for forty years. Now I've come to my second death. It's a beautiful summer. The very old people say it's the best they remember. I'm lucky but I can't hope to live nine lives. The islands change colour all the time. In the evening they're dark. They're called the eyes of the sea. Why should I mind them? They're not my life. This house is my life. My mother was its first housekeeper and I would have been its second. I came here as a servant. Now I live here by right. I could have died on the island. I was saved – not even by a friend but by an enemy. That's how lucky I was! When the house was made into flats people said I should be caretaker. I went on the town council and served there till this summer. We built a clinic and a school and houses. Now I sit on the terrace and watch the sea. During the day as the shadow moves over the stones I move my chair to stay in the sun. When David was studying he put his table in front of his window where the sun fell on it. As it moved he moved his chair so that he read and made his notes in the sun. When I mind my neighbour's children I put them on the floor and they crawl to the sun. They cry at the dark but no one cries at the light. That's what I've learned. I have no memory of the islands to drive me out of the sun to cry in my cave.

XENIA: You're right. Don't be frightened of bogeymen. (*Automatically glances at her empty glass.*) No, it's too early. (*To* ANN:) I haven't been on the island for years. Ask David to take us in his boat.

VOICE (*off, calls*): Ivan.

ANN: Who's Ivan?

XENIA: All the men here are called Ivan.

XENIA *goes.*

MARTHE: Two girls arm in arm are calling a young man in a rowing boat.

TWO VOICES (*off, call*): Ivan.

ANN: Has he heard?

MARTHE: Yes. They're waving to each other. (*Stands behind* ANN *and puts her hands on her shoulders and raises them over her head in the gesture of lifting the baby.*) When we were young parents took their new babies down to the rocks on a sunny day, held them over their heads and shouted their names to the sea. It was a custom.

FOUR

The island. A sandy floor before a rock wall.
XENIA *sits alone.*
A GERMAN *comes on.*

GERMAN: Speak German?

XENIA: Yes.

GERMAN: Good. Your boat is tied up at the mooring. Please take me back to the hotel.

XENIA: Is your boat lost?

GERMAN: My son and daughter-in-law dropped me on the island and went for a trip along the coast. They should have been back two hours ago. I can't see their boat on the water. They've made me late for the evening meal. When you take the pension with full board you must come to the restaurant for the evening meal by eight-thirty. It is better to be there at seven-thirty. Then there is time to ask for seconds.

XENIA: Your son and daughter-in-law will come back. They'll worry if you're not here.

GERMAN: That will teach them to make their elders wait. If I'm late I won't be served with the evening meal. The waiters are stern with those who come late. They want to go home.

XENIA: My friend will take you in his boat. Wait at the landing. No, sit in the boat under the awning.

GERMAN: Have they left you on your own? Our young people! I don't complain. Sigi could not be a more dutiful son. His Haidi is like my daughter. Since my wife died I would be lonely without them. They take me on holiday every year. I haven't seen you at the hotel.

XENIA: I stay with friends.

GERMAN: O, friends are better than a hotel. The young people are not married?

XENIA: No.

GERMAN: I see them often. The other day I saw them on the rocks. The young man talked to the girl and tried to press himself on her. Our young people!

XENIA: If you care to wait in the boat.

GERMAN: O, I said something to shock. You have no reason to complain about the young lady. That is a good daughter. She pushed the young man away.

XENIA: Thank you. I would like to be on my –

GERMAN: You are right. It's wrong for the elders to tell the young people what to do. Sometimes they set us a good example. They remind us we're still young and on holiday! I saw them just now from the mouth of the ammunition cave. They went down the other side of the island. You can't see so far from the cave. If you are concerned for the young lady I shall wander down and pretend to look for something I have lost.

XENIA: You were here in the war.

GERMAN: Ja. I said ammunition cave. That gave me away. You know what happened here in the war?

XENIA: Yes, I lived here.

GERMAN: Ah, that war. Terrible. Terrible. Terrible. So much killing. (*He calls:*) Sigi! Haidi! (*To* XENIA:) Haidi is a sensible girl and Sigi has a good underwater watch but they lose all sense of time. They didn't go off to enjoy themselves without me. They think I want to be on my own for a while. It's their way to be kind. It would have been good to come back with comrades and talk of the old days. These islands were a camp. Prisoners were routed on. Terrible times. Tcha. But we must make the best of it. Even in the end – till the very last days – we went to the bars in the evenings to drink a glass of wine and sing the old songs. I carried my accordion all through the war till I got back to Germany. I had to barter it for food. Ruins and blackmarket, that's all that was left. There was no music in my life for years. But we recovered. The spirit inside was not broken. That is what counts. You have a grudge against us?

XENIA: You destroyed our lives.

GERMAN: No no, the old days were over. No one was strong enough to save them. Now we must learn to live in a new world. When I got back all my people were dead. The elders, aunts, my brother, even my girl. My family took her in when she was bombed out. They all died together in one house. After the war I married her sister. I have a good

job. I sell refrigerators. I can give you a discount. You
could bring it over the border.

XENIA: I live in England.

GERMAN: Ah, you married an Englander. It is sad not to live
in your own country. I'll tell you a secret. Do you know
where we are? Guess. This spot. That was the execution
wall.

XENIA: O.

GERMAN: In Germany we would put a statue there. We have
many artists. When prisoners were shot the lizards jumped
into the cracks and stayed there till we left. Then they came
to sit in the sun. You have something to eat in your
bag?

XENIA: Yes.

GERMAN: There are butter marks on the paper. Today we
had lunch early so the children could have full use of the
boat. You must hire one for the day. Not cheap. If you
don't eat here the sun makes you ill. I learned that from the
war.

XENIA (*food*): Please eat this. It's left from our lunch.

GERMAN: Ah, sandwich. How English. (*He eats.*) Good.
Thank you. It is better to be kind than make terrible wars.
But it had to be.

XENIA: Were you here long?

GERMAN: For the duration. There's nothing to hide. We
were questioned after the war. By GI Jonny. This wasn't
a concentration camp. We were private soldiers: not
officers, not Gestapo, not guilty. We garrisoned the town,
guarded the roads, kept the prisoners. When we took them
to be questioned we handed them over at the door. It had to
be. The civvies killed us and our officers. Not in fair play
you understand. They crept up on our sentries at night and
cut their throats with a knife. People who do these things
must be dealt with. Poor bastards. I was sorry for them. I
did nothing they wouldn't have done to me. Crumbs fall

into your hair when you eat sandwiches naked. (*He laughs and brushes crumbs from his chest.*)

XENIA: You didn't kill anyone.

GERMAN: O yes. Sometimes. When it was urgent. It was forbidden to be questioned or killed on this island. Prisoners were taken to the little island first. To begin with regulations were strictly enforced. But what can you do when prisoners are sitting in the boats and there is no petrol for the engines? You can row them across but it's hard. There are so many prisoners. So organisation broke down and discipline became lax: we knew the end was coming. We started to shoot prisoners here. There was such disorganisation it could even happen that ammunition ran out. Headquarters gave the order: hostages. There is no alternative. It is easy to say hostages, it's not so easy to say ammunition. Many times our CO had to go on the scrounge. He was called a scrounger as if he cadged cigarettes. No, he was a generous man. But the officers fell out and swore at each other. Not the behaviour of gentlemen. Bad blood between comrades. The batmen and clerks told us everything. Commander Lauber said: 'If you want to play the hero and get a medal for shooting people use your own ammunition'. That's how things were. How could we win a war like that? They tried to sink them in ships. But we ran out of ships. The fishermen sank theirs before we could get them. We needed ours to patrol the coast. So that was called off. Yes, it's good to remember how hard things were. At one time many people were buried on this island. They were killed here so where could we put them? In a war bodies are a problem even to Germans. Take them to the mainland? More work, porters, boats, more lorries to take them from the quay to the hills. Throw them into the sea? No tide. The beaches are fouled. The town can't go about its business. You would think this was the devil's island it was so difficult for our adjutant to run. Now I will tell you about the end. When we had to go home. By then the island was full of bodies. They had been sealed up in caves and pushed down cracks. The soldiers said if the island was a coat the pockets would bulge! The order came: exhume the dead and throw them into the sea. We were angry. It would seem as if we had something to hide. Our enemies were quick to lie about us. We were not criminals. We'd done everything in the open. According to laws of war. Harsh – but war is harsh. Now we must open the graves. Dig the bodies out of the rocks. It is an order. We stood guard while the prisoners dug and carried. Such stench. Can you imagine? For three days. The bodies were thrown into the sea. But there is no tide. The bodies won't go away. The sea will not take them. It is as if it was against us. They floated round the island. Only a few were skele-tons. Sand had preserved the skin of the rest. They drifted on the surface or just below it. Some of them held hands – that's how they died. When we went to the land for sup-plies – O the evenings of songs in the bars were over by then – our boats towed the bodies behind us in our wakes as if they were swimming after us and pointing at us with their outstretched hands – that's how they died. A dead woman clutched a child in the crook of her arm and floated on top of the sea as if she held the child up out of the water to see us. The public address system played dance music to keep spirits high. We came with marches and left with waltzes. (*He walks away.*) Where are those bad children? I was lucky to find someone to speak German. This is my first time in your country since the war. Haidi and Sigi brought me here as a surprise. Other years we went to Majorca. Malta. Spain. Italy twice. Majorca six times. Majorca is best for a holiday. The Crusader Hotel is excel-lent. Reasonable terms. So is the hotel here. And it's new. It works. Next year nothing will work. Yes, I remember those days well. We cut our initials and army numbers in the rock. Now they're gone. The wind erases them with a handful of sand. But it couldn't have done it so soon. It's not so strong. Hooligans did it. And put their initials in our place. You are quiet, madam. Is it the sun? Have I eaten your food? I think my stories upset you. This was not one of the bad camps. In the bad camps people were burned. Some of their guards collapsed with fatigue. They were transferred to us here. This was a good posting by the sea. They said that in those places so much fat hung in the air you covered your coffee with your hand and drank from beneath it. It even got into their skin so they didn't smell of themselves anymore. They smelt of other people. Or like the dead. When they were on leave their wives thought they were in bed with a stranger. Ho hoo! That's an army for you! Take the clothes off your back and put you in uniform. Take your name and give you a number. Take your head and stuff it with orders. Then take your skin – and you end up smelling of someone else. (*He points.*) Is that bread? Talking is good for the appetite. I mustn't be greedy. Even if Sigi came now we'd be late for the restaurant. If we go there one minute late they turn us away. The young ones spoil me. I can have what I want at the bar. I say no, such extravagance is a waste. Why pay for food you don't eat? Between us we'd lose three meals. The hotel doesn't lose. Tomorrow the kitchen serves our steaks as casserole.

XENIA (*food*): Please take it.

GERMAN (*eating*): Good. Thank you. Crept up on our sentries with a knife. Slick.

XENIA: We killed as many of you as we could.

GERMAN: Of course, of course. Natural after the rumours that spread about us. People like to believe the worst.

XENIA: I know what happened. (*She points.*) I lived over there.

GERMAN (*laughs*): We were that close? I sailed under those cliffs many times. You see that big house? Our officers dined there. In the war there was a young girl, the daughter of the house. We called her the girl in white. She stood on the terrace and pretended to stare at the sea. Hour after hour for days at a time. We sang to her as we sailed below or swam. We watched her through binoculars. Our comrades' throats were cut. They said it was quieter than shooting – but that's how they liked to do it. We loved her, we were young soldiers. She never smiled or waved. She dared not. The partisans would have shot her. But she was our friend. She stood there as a sign. It was all she could do.

XENIA: I don't understand!

GERMAN: We didn't come here as enemies. We were defenders. Could we have done all we did out of hate? No, our officers said: we acted in honour. To save you from scum.

XENIA: What nonsense!

GERMAN: You see! Our officers were right: all that blood and suffering and nothing is learned. Europe was threatened. Civilization, Beethoven, art. What else is there? Americans and pygmies.

XENIA: She didn't stand there for your sake! I expect she was lonely! So many young men were killed! She wondered how long she had to live.

GERMAN: Men are animals. We can't be trusted with another man's wife or his money. Not even with our own daughters. No one's safe on our streets at night. If we don't get our fodder we whine. What saves us from ourselves? Culture. The standards of our fathers. They struggled for centuries to make them strong. But standards are always as weak as the girl in white. Always. The animal wants to be on top. If that happens we're lost. The apes come out of their jungle. That's why we went to war.

XENIA: You're talking nonsense!

GERMAN: The girl in white could tell you!

XENIA: You invade us, bomb us, rob us – for our good!

GERMAN: That was because you listened to scum. If we'd listened to scum Europe would be a labour camp. If you'd helped us there'd be more hope for the world. Instead you'll see what happens. The jungles are open.

XENIA: Go away.

GERMAN: I can show you the truth. There was a woman who worked for the girl on the balcony. Servant. She was taken hostage: more throats had been cut. The girl asked our commander to let her go. Now parents had begged us for their children on the streets. Tried to climb on the lorries to take their place. We pushed them off. But our commander gave that servant back to the girl. We weren't angry for our dead comrades. Some of us had tears in our eyes. That girl had a right to ask for anything. We were at war for her. What happens to our culture, our way of life, when people like that go? She came from the same class as our officers. She knew that – and what it meant. It was proved when she came and asked for the woman. She needn't have asked, she could have given an order! I wish I could meet her and thank her for all she did for us. It was not to be. When we left her class were shot or chased out. They put some of them in our old huts.

XENIA: How dare you! Who are you? Who told you to say these things to me? Someone paid you!

GERMAN: Ah, you're one of those who benefited from the pickings. You did well out of the end of the war so you see it from that point of view.

XENIA (*picks up her bag*): Go away!

GERMAN: O madam, don't be angry. Thank you for the sandwich. The heat. My empty stomach. I rambled on. Yes, but I will not be humiliated even if I stay on this island all night – at my age that would not be easy. I came here in my prime. I risked my life. The sacrifice of young manhood should be respected. Our young people would have to do all we did if those times come again. It would have to be.

XENIA: Wait here. My daughter's friend will take you in his boat.

GERMAN: It's better if I wait on board. You said under the shade.

XENIA: Don't follow me!

GERMAN: Your friend will leave in a hurry without me.

XENIA: Stop following me! I shall report you to the police!

XENIA *goes.*

GERMAN (*shouting after her*): My dear lady, I didn't touch you! O dear, Sigi and Haidi are drowned! (*He starts to follow* XENIA.) Haidi wouldn't let him be rash –

XENIA (off): Go away!

GERMAN: – but he doesn't know these waters. The rocks are dangerous. It would be terrible to go home alone.

The GERMAN *goes.* ANN *and* DAVID *come on. They wear swimming clothes. Ann has a light blue wrap.*

DAVID: This island is sacred to us. I won't make love to another girl here. Why am I so happy? From now on we have a secret power: whenever we're angry or sad we'll think of this and it will make us happy. We have fallen in love. You won't stay here. Instead I shall plant a pine in the place where we were today. I'll water it till it grows tall and strong. I'll scatter seed under it so that flocks of birds come there to live. (*Calmly.*) This is the wall where my mother was to be shot. Look at the fossils and veins of quartz and bullet marks in the rock. When they shot simple people – not fighters or hardened politicians but children and old women – they dragged the dead out of sight so that the simple people wouldn't know where they were and run away. There was blood on the ground – but there was

blood on all the rocks on the island and on the walls of the
rooms. So they thought there was still time for a plane to
come out of the sky, or a hand – or a friendly boat to appear
on the sea. That was at the start of the war. After a time
they made even the simple people climb over the bodies to
the wall. If they stumbled they clubbed them. The
Assyrian has said I will make him more dead than he was
before. The Spaniard has said I will kill the dead twice.

The GERMAN *comes in.*

GERMAN: Speak German?

DAVID: Yes.

GERMAN: Thank god. That is your boat, sir. Goodday, miss.
Please take me to the hotel.

DAVID: Are you stranded?

GERMAN: Sigi hired a boat to surprise Haidi. Now they're
lost. I must get back for the evening meal. The door of the
restaurant is shut at eight-thirty sharp. If you tap on the
glass the waiters look away and the guests hold up the food
on their forks and laugh. You can't get the manager, he's
cleaning the pool.

DAVID: You can come with us.

GERMAN: Thank you, thank you. I sweat with anxiety. You
must not let the lady attack me. I didn't touch her. Sigi and
Haidi will be cross. The lady in Ibiza had too much sun oil
on her leg. The sand set in the crease. I brushed it off. I
don't want any scandal. Because I'm German the older
generation – it's natural.

DAVID: I'll take you in my boat.

GERMAN: We work for our holiday. You too. A song in the
evening and a glass of wine. I wanted it all to go well today.
Three weeks pass so quickly. Tomorrow we go back to
Bächelstein. Tonight I wanted to buy a special bottle of
wine. Yesterday was Sigi and Haidi's turn. That's how we
end our holidays. A toast to the next year.

DAVID: Don't be distressed. Wait in the boat.

GERMAN: The lady is angry. I'll wait on the path. Not to go to the boat till you come? When you pass me on the way down I'll follow you. The lady must not say such things. I don't molest ladies.

The GERMAN *goes out.*

DAVID: Ann. Death creates desire. Lust. The stupid think that's perverse. No. Lust isn't drawn to death. When life sees death it become strong itself, it *will* be strong. While we cry our distorted mouth reaches for one that smiles. You won't stay here – but we'll sleep together every night till you go away. I will plant a great treasure of seed in you to carry abroad to your own country. *There* you will bear a child! The child and that pine are the only things we can give to my mother – or all who die.

ANN: A tense woman sitting upright in a corner of a boat. A hungry old man squatting in the dust halfway down to the landing place. They each have their own thoughts. Angry, offended, waiting for planes, suspecting waiters, staring at their watches. The stranger should be grateful he met us. My mother is angry because we made her wait while we went to the other side of the island. I don't wish to make her angry but it doesn't matter if she is. 'The gods love the widespread races of happy man and willingly lengthen the days of his fleeting life, to share with him the joyful view from their unchanging sky, for a brief span of time.' They're on the edge of the island waiting to leave. We're free and told to be happy. Let's sit here a little longer.

FIVE

The house. Night.
Empty.
XENIA *comes on. She taps on* MARTHE'*s door.*

XENIA: Can I speak to you? (*Slight pause.*) You're not asleep.
I looked into your room from the garden.

XENIA *walks away from the door. After a moment*
MARTHE *comes out.*

MARTHE: Yes?
XENIA: I must speak to you.
MARTHE: Can't it wait till morning? (*No answer.*) Move my
chair. There's a breeze.

XENIA *puts* MARTHE'*s chair stage centre.* MARTHE *sits*
in it.

XENIA: David and Ann are out.
MARTHE: Dancing at the hotel. Does it shock you?
XENIA: It's not my concern. No doubt he wouldn't dance if
he thought you cared. Shall I come here when you're dead?
MARTHE: That doesn't concern me.
XENIA: I'll do what you want.
MARTHE: Live your own life
XENIA: You might wish me to come. I'd keep your memory
alive: I knew you so well.
MARTHE: Do as you please.
XENIA: Have I ever shown you any resentment?
MARTHE: I'm tired now.
XENIA: I was an only child. When my father died this house
– all he had – would have been mine. It was taken from me
even before he died. Some of the people who took it had
been with us for years. Your son thinks if I was here he'd be

blacking boots. It shows even when he smiles. My father sent clever children to the university whatever their background. Paid their tuition fees, bought their books, clothed some of them, gave them an allowance –

MARTHE: What d'you want to say?

XENIA: – but I've never held a grudge.

MARTHE: No.

XENIA: Then why do you despise me?

MARTHE: I don't.

XENIA: So does your son. Only he's more offensive because he has no excuse. I'm tired of being abused and attacked.

MARTHE: If you have a complaint about David make it to him. I'm sorry if he's been rude to you. He's young and thoughtless.

XENIA: He thinks I want to come back here. I knew that life couldn't go on. I was hated and resented even when I was a child. If I'd had to spend my life like that I'd be old and embittered now. Instead I have a good husband, my daughter and kind friends. There's my shop. I sell the best clothes as cheaply as I can and have the pleasure of seeing young people enjoying life. At their age we could have been shot. Many of our friends were. D'you seriously think I want to go back to all that? Life has been good to me. And there's nothing I need blame myself for. Whatever my family did Marthe I was young when I left – for *those* days little more than a child. Yet you despise me.

MARTHE: No.

XENIA: Don't you know you do? Your condition's worse than I thought. It's a disease you don't even know you've got. That's why you've passed it on to your son. Has he got to live with it after you're dead? D'you want to ruin his life? Can't we get rid of the past even now? Let's sit here quietly till he comes and then the three of us will talk.

MARTHE: What about?

XENIA: O Marthe you wrong yourself! You know. My

daughter told you how much I keep secret. I never tell her things that would shame anyone she knew. But if this is to be your last summer, then at least we two should be honest with each other. I saved your life. Yet you gave evidence against us. Not out of fear. You weren't forced. My father might have been shot. How wrong. Such guilt is almost unforgiveable.

MARTHE: What guilt? Let us talk about ourselves. People in my generation had to depend on your family in order to live. But why should that have been? Your kindness made us beggars. It made some of us grateful, which was worse. There can never be enough kindness to make the world human. If you spent your life being kind people would still die of ignorance and neglect. Much more is needed. Let's leave it till the morning. Years ago your father's bank was robbed and a girl cashier shot. The man who did it hid on the island. Your father saw him through his binoculars and went out in his motor-boat. A group of men were standing beside him at the wheel. The young man saw them and realized he'd been discovered. He jumped into the water and swam for the shore. Your father chased him. He turned and swam towards the open sea. He was that desperate. When your father's men dragged him on board he struggled like a madman to get back in the water. They had to tie him up and lay him on the bottom of the boat as if he was a corpse. Did your father rescue him from drowning or catch a fish for dinner? While that went on your mother and her ladies took tea on the terrace. They weren't a vulgar mob, they didn't line the railings to cheer. They quietly drank their tea. If your father had brought the man here your mother would have given him tea and wrapped him in her stole. Would that have made his punishment easier to bear? The foundations of your world were crooked and so everything in it was crooked. Your kindness, consideration, consistency were meaningless. All the good you did was meaningless. In your world the good did evil. What could be worse? Most of us spent our life swimming out to the open sea. The confusion and competition led to such panic and madness that in the end there was war. The soldiers on the island didn't have much excuse for not seeing the blood they shed. But your state was worse. You had every excuse for what you did: your hands were clean! Your world was a puppet show. You thought the puppets moved because of the little pieces of wood under their bright coats. They were moved by strings: the factories, banks, governments that control our lives. What we do, what we are, depends on the relationship between us and such things. Faced with that kindness is like blowing on a storm to make it go away. But when those relations are just we will live justly. Kindness will have its meaning. Justice and mercy will be one.

XENIA: You remember what you choose! My father was a liberal man. When that thief was sentenced to death he used his newspaper to get him reprieved. The dead girl's family came here to abuse him. I had to be taken out for a walk so I didn't hear the vile things they said. The fascists demonstrated. Their party membership doubled. Father resisted them. We were happy when that man was saved!

MARTHE: I can't say any more. Your father was as kind as you. He could afford his halo. The young man was grateful to him. When the war came he volunteered to fight for your father's world and was shot. It seems to me people like you live backwards. You learn nothing. You spend your life burrowing through the ground to your grave. Well, you have no more power. That's what matters.

XENIA: Now you admit you despise me.

MARTHE (*as if* XENIA *were not there*): How do you live through the last moments? The last hour in hospital. Walking out of the cell. Perhaps I should have stayed in the hut when you came. I could have helped the others. Put my

arms round the old women or helped the girls who stumbled. I might even have sung. I wanted to fly into the line of
light under the door. Then the door opened. I'd secretly
begged for life. Not hoped, calculated. (*Smiles at* XENIA.)
I knew you'd come. I left them to die alone – as I am now.
They're dead, the huts are burned, the island's free. It
hasn't changed for me. I saw a photograph of my death. I
lived my second life in a new way. I listen to them not you.

XENIA: You shouldn't. They're dead and you're not. When I
was a student you were a servant. I envied you. You had
more dignity, more intelligence, than the rest of us. Now
our roles are reversed. I got away – but you're corrupted by
the past.

> XENIA *goes. Music starts in the distance.* MARTHE *doesn't
> react.* XENIA *returns.*

The discotheque. Now I shan't sleep.

MARTHE: It stops after midnight.

XENIA: I'd better take you to your room.

MARTHE: I'm all right.

XENIA: I shan't come here again. My husband told me not
to. This is my grave. They say in prison my father's hair
turned white in a week. I didn't see him. I should have
drowned myself when they took him away. Gone down the
rocks in the dark and slipped into the sea. Now it's too late.
They'd say 'A bitter old woman'. I'm not. It's just that you
took everything from me – and still want more!

MARTHE: What could I want? Go to your room. It's quieter
on your side of the house. (*To herself:*) I spent so much of
my life in struggle. Lost so many friends. New clothes
become old when I put them on. I'm worn out. I listen to
the air going in and out of my body. Like footsteps in a
corridor. It's not easy: it's as if a crowd had to die.

XENIA (*to herself*): The world was taken away from me. They
threw the furniture out of the house and left me in the

emptiness. I can't begin again. I've spent years pointing at
my dead body – and no one sees it.

MARTHE: Yes, you can't begin. You belong to a family who
die in prisons. The old woman beside me. Gripped the
bench with both hands. Her knuckles shone like a child's.
'If I could live to spit in her face.' (MARTHE *heaves herself
out of her chair, spits in* XENIA's *face and falls back on the
floor.*) It's gone.

XENIA: How dare you! Because you're dying you think you
can be a monster! Oh you must feel better! You carried a
dead woman's spit round in your mouth for forty years! I
shan't sleep here. I'll go to the hotel. Send my things on in
the morning. I won't trouble you to give a message to my
daughter. I'll write a note.

XENIA *goes.* MARTHE *doesn't move.* XENIA *returns.*

Are you all right? If you wish I'll help you to your room.

MARTHE: Go away.

XENIA: It's clear you're not well. The drugs you take have
affected you. I don't want to be accused of letting you die of
exposure. No doubt your son would give evidence against
me.

XENIA *goes to* MARTHE.

MARTHE: Get out.

XENIA: As you wish. I'll leave you to suffer the consequences
of your stubbornness.

XENIA *goes.* MARTHE *goes to her room and tries the
handle of the door. She can't turn it. For a moment she rests
on the wall. She tries the handle again. The door opens.*
MARTHE *goes into her room and shuts the door behind her.*

SIX

The house. Morning.
MARTHE *comes up from the street with a pot of petunias.*
She puts it on the floor. She goes out and returns with a
folded table. She opens it. She goes out. She returns with a
chair on which there are a cloth and a tray of breakfast
things. She begins to lay the table for breakfast. ANN *comes*
in.

ANN: Good morning.

MARTHE: Good morning. How are you?

ANN: Fine. And you? I have mother's note. You two have quarrelled.

MARTHE: It's nothing.

ANN: What was it about?

MARTHE: It's finished.

ANN: Really, you behave like children. Mother is difficult but she wouldn't leave without a reason.

MARTHE: Please ask her.

ANN: O Marthe! (*She sighs.*) I suppose you're upset. Was it about David and me?

MARTHE: I made this jam. A neighbour gave me some plums from her tree. The big woman. You've seen her child playing with her apron while she hangs out her washing.

ANN: I'll lay the table.

MARTHE: I'll do it.

ANN: It's so much nonsense. You make me cross. Are you quarrelling with me now?

MARTHE: Don't be rude. Laying the table is one of the few jobs I can still do. I covered the table with a clean cloth and brought a pot of petunias from the roof. Hand me the plates. (*They lay the table together.*) Was there a storm last night?

ANN: No.

MARTHE: I dreamed I went to sleep and in the night a door banged in the wind. I woke up and listened to the sea. I must have been sleeping all the time. This morning everything looks as if it had been in a storm. Dust and bits of paper and rubbish blown away. Boxes and tins blown to the sides of the houses. The leaves are still crooked from the wind. The town looks as battered and new as a child that's cried itself to sleep.

ANN: There wasn't a storm.

MARTHE: No, I dreamed it. Give me the knives.

MARTHE *lays the table.*

I'll set a place for your mother. I don't think she'll come, but she might and it would be better if she found a place set for her. Perhaps she'll come to breakfast tomorrow. Or perhaps she won't. Fetch the coffee and milk from the kitchen. The petunia needs water.

ANN: I'm hungry.

MARTHE: Wait for David.

ANN: He's asleep.

MARTHE: Wake him. Is he a good lover?

ANN: Yes.

MARTHE: The three of us will eat together. I'll cut the bread.

ANN: Marthe. Your ankle's swollen.

MARTHE: It began in the night. I found it like that this morning.

ANN: It must hurt.

MARTHE: No. I stood on it too long. I'll rest it later. Don't tell David. He'll give me more tablets. Pass my wrap. (ANN *gives* MARTHE *her shawl. Looking at the sea:*) The sea is calm and the water's piled up as if it has been in the storm. Everything's open and new. (*Coffee cup.*) There's a stain in this cup. Take it into the kitchen and wash it.

ANN: It's nothing. I'll drink from it.

MARTHE: No. Wash it. Respect things. Use them properly.

> ANN *goes.* MARTHE *wraps herself in her shawl and cuts bread.*

What will you do if your mother asks you to move to the hotel? It's lonely to be on your own. I'd hate it.

ANN (*off*): You weren't *that* horrible to her. The quarrel is between you.

MARTHE (*slightly amused*): She'll say I stole her daughter.

> ANN *comes back with coffee, milk, the cup and water for the petunia.*

ANN: She knows if I stay it's because I want to.

MARTHE: Pour the milk in a jug. (*She pours.*) A jug to make the table beautiful.

ANN: You're making washing-up.

MARTHE: Good. I won't see many more beautiful things. You'll be sad for a few days and then your life will go on again. It will be beautiful. You'll think of me with fondness. Put a chair in front of each place.

ANN: How d'you know it will be beautiful?

> ANN *goes out.*

MARTHE (*working*): What's more useless than death? Life without death would be. How could you find anything beautiful if you looked at it forever? You'd grow tired of it. Why fall in love if it lasted forever? When you'd forgiven yourselves a thousand times you'd tire of forgiveness. You'd grow tired of changing the people you loved. (ANN *returns with three folded chairs, opens them and sets them at the table.*) If you ate for eternity why bother to taste what you're eating? You can taste the next meal. When you've cried for one mistake you wouldn't cry for the next. You'd

have eternity to put it right. Soon your eyes would be full of
sleep. You'd go deaf. You wouldn't listen to voices because
they would give you the trouble of answering. Why listen
to them? It would be useless to know which was a sparrow
or a waterfall. In eternity there would be no future. You'd
sit on the ground and turn to stone. Dust would pile up and
bury you. If we didn't die we'd live like the dead. Without
death there's no life. No beauty, love or happiness. You
can't laugh for more than a few hours or weep more than a
few days. No one could bear more than one life. Only hell
could be eternal. Sometimes life is cruel and death is
sudden – that's the price we pay for not being stones. Don't
let the lightning strike you or madmen burn your house.
Don't give yourself to your enemies or neglect anyone in
need. Fight. But in the end death is a friend who brings a
gift: life. Not for you but the others. I die so that you might
live. Did you call David? Breakfast's ready.

ANN: I didn't dry the cup.

MARTHE: Let me.

ANN *goes and* MARTHE *dries the cup. She smooths a corner
of the table with her hand, goes to a chair at the table, pulls
the wrap round her legs and sleeps. The* GERMAN *comes up
from the street. He carries a bunch of flowers wrapped in
florist's cellophane and tied with yellow ribbon.*

GERMAN: Speak German? ... Dear Lady. (*He coughs.*) The
taxi is taking us to the airport. If we miss the plane ... It's
part of the package. (*He touches* MARTHE's *wrist. No
response. He wanders round the terrace. Calls louder, to the
house.*) Hello. (*To* MARTHE.) Pst! (*To himself:*) Tch tch. If
I wake the lady will she be angry?

VOICE (*off, calls*): Vati!

GERMAN (*calls*): Soon! There's a good girl, Haidi! (*He
smacks his hands together as if reprimanding a child and calls:*)
Shush! (*He turns to* MARTHE:) The children are cross. I

insisted to come up. Now the taxi's ticking over. The driver will charge extra. Sigi will sulk on the plane. (*Slightly tearfully.*) Only to press her hand . . .

Absent-mindedly he goes to the table, spreads jam on bread and eats it. Off, a car horn. He puts the flowers down and goes. DAVID *comes in. He wears a dressing-gown. He goes to the railing and looks at the sea.* ANN *comes in.*

ANN: I thought I heard a call.
DAVID (*grunt*): Who?
ANN (*to* MARTHE): Marthe.
DAVID: Let her sleep.
ANN: She wanted to eat with us.
DAVID (*goes to the table and sits*): She ate some bread. Not taken her tablet.

ANN *sits.* DAVID *pours coffee.*

ANN: She wouldn't tell me what they rowed about.
DAVID (*looks at his watch*): Your mother will.
ANN: Are you late?
DAVID: No.
ANN (*takes coffee*): Thank you.
DAVID: Don't go to the hotel.
ANN: I must see how my –
DAVID: To stay.
ANN: O no, how could I?
DAVID: I don't want to come between you and her. She'll have you all the time when you're gone.
ANN: She's not an ogress. She's kind if you let her.
DAVID: All things under the sun throw a shadow. Your mother throws hers towards the light.
ANN: Flowers. (*She picks up the flowers.*) A delivery man. That's who I heard.
DAVID: Are they for you?

ANN: The envelope's written in German. (*She gives it to* DAVID.)

DAVID (*reads. Looks up*): For you. 'An das schöne Fräulein in weiss.' To the beautiful girl in white.

ANN: How amazing.

DAVID: You wear white.

ANN: Sometimes.

DAVID: Expensive.

ANN *opens the envelope, takes out a letter and gives it to* DAVID.

DAVID (*reads*): Merciful lady – (*He looks up.*) A common form of address in the German tongue. (*He reads.*) I could not end our holiday in your beautiful homeland without writing this letter. Not till after dinner on that memorable day did I realise I had again met the beautiful girl – (ANN *tries to snatch the letter,* DAVID *runs round the table reading,* ANN *chases him laughing*) – in white we gazed on so long ago. Believe an old but still active man when he speaks from the heart of the great debt he owes you. Merciful lady I understand why you did not speak to me on the boat. Happily you now understand the cause of my disrespect. When I deliver these flowers I shall press your hand in silence and let them speak for me. (DAVID *stops* ANN *with a gesture.*) You will be gratified to learn that Sigi and Haidi are safe. Their boat ran out of petrol. Friendly fishermen took them in tow. Alas there will be no time to present them to you. I have told them of our memorable meeting and will do so again many times in the years ahead. To the beautiful girl in white on the balcony of long ago with the humble respects of her dutiful Heinrich Hemmel. P.S. I am innocent. (*He stops reading.*) With an address.

ANN: They're for my mother. Some old flame. The balcony of long ago. What can it mean?

DAVID: The German we took in the boat. Put them in water.

ANN *goes out.* DAVID *takes a tablet and glass of water to* MARTHE. *He puts the tablet and glass on the floor. He feels her pulse. He kneels in front of her.* XENIA *comes in. She carries a light jacket.*

XENIA: David.

DAVID *presses* MARTHE's *hands against his face, kisses them and covers his hands with them.*

DAVID: She's warm. Her hands are still warm.

ANN *comes back with a large blue vase.* DAVID *begins to cry.*

Still warm. Give me something to cover her hands. Keep her warmth in. Don't let it go! Let me feel her warmth!
XENIA (*to* ANN): Is she – ?
DAVID: Help me! Anything! Anything! Her warmth will go!

ANN *takes* XENIA's *jacket and gives it to* DAVID. *He covers* MARTHE's *hands with it and presses his head against it.*

XENIA: I'm sorry. We had a quarrel. After a dreadful day on the island.
ANN: Go back to the hotel.
XENIA: No no I must stay. There are things to do. You'll need me.
ANN: Wait there. I'll come to you. Your flowers. (*She gives them to* XENIA.)
XENIA: Don't push me like that!
ANN: Please mother!
XENIA: As you wish. I'll send for my things. I won't put you to that trouble. You'll have enough to do.
ANN: Go on. I'll come soon. I won't be long.
XENIA: Stay here. I don't need you. I telephoned Daddy last night to say I'd come home today. Of course I'll stay for the

funeral. What are these ugly flowers? (*She gives the flowers back to* ANN.) I'm sorry she's dead. I came to tell her I wasn't angry. My presence filled her with a great rage. It was bad for someone in her condition. If I'd known I'd never have come here.

> XENIA *goes.*
> DAVID *lifts* MARTHE *from the chair. Her feet are off the ground.* ANN *watches for a moment and then goes.* DAVID *presses* MARTHE's *hands to his head.*

DAVID: Bless me. Bless me. Still warm...

> DAVID *lowers* MARTHE *to her knees and kneels before her. He presses her hands to his eyes and cries.*

SEVEN
[The Agreement]

The house. Day.
MARTHE's *chair has been taken away.*
ANN *sits at the table and mechanically drinks coffee.*
DAVID *comes in.*

ANN: Shouldn't you lie down?
DAVID: No.
ANN: I'll come and hold you.
DAVID: I'm all right.

He sits at the table.

I've seen so many deaths. I cried for them all this morning.

> ANN *pours coffee. He takes it but doesn't drink.*

ANN: I shall go back to England soon. I must find a new job.
DAVID: Perhaps we deceived ourselves. There may be no child.

ANN: I don't know yet.

DAVID: If there is will you keep it?

ANN: Yes.

DAVID: Alone?

ANN: If I have to.

DAVID: You must tell it I'm its father.

ANN: If it grew up I'd bring it to you. Mother must go to the funeral.

DAVID (*drinks coffee*): If you weren't here I'd say no. It's as you please.

ANN: Did she say where her ashes were to be thrown?

DAVID (*smiles*): In the garden.

Fables

Contents

Certain Stories

A man was walking alone on a street at night in Morocco. He did not know the city. There were groups of young men about but because he did not know the city he called the groups gangs. A man overtook him. He wore a dark suit. He stopped in front of him, turned to face him and blocked his way. The man in the dark suit said 'Would you like me to kill you?' He did not speak in anger or violence. He sounded as if he wished to help. Of course the other man sidestepped and hurried on. The man in the black suit followed him. Again he overtook him, stopped and turned to block his way and without any apparent offence he asked 'Would you like me to kill you?' Again the other man hurried on. He didn't run because he was afraid of attracting attention. Perhaps some of the men would come from the gangs to help the man in the black suit. A third time the man followed him, overtook him, stopped, turned, blocked his way and asked the question and the man hurried on. This time the man in the black suit did not follow him and he got safely back to his hotel.

When I was told this story I was with friends. They began to explain the story. Perhaps 'to kill' was a code. Perhaps it meant 'Would you like some drugs?' Perhaps the man in the black suit was homosexual and had said kiss not kill and the other man had misheard because he was tense. Perhaps it was a special local invitation. Perhaps it meant a visit to certain brothels. Perhaps the killing was symbolic. Or a fantasy. Perhaps the other man had misunderstood altogether. And so on. These explanations spoiled the story for me. They explained it but gave it no meaning.

Suppose the word had been misheard or misunderstood – what follows from that? The point is that the man could walk on the street and believe he heard such a word. Perhaps this tells us more not about Morocco but about Manchester or Chicago. What is interesting is that the mystery of the story throws so much light on reality. We should avoid confusion and mystification but that does not mean that stories should not be left to make their own points.

The Dragon

There was once a dragon who breathed fire. Everyone chased him through the streets because they said that breathing fire was bad. He tried to hide in a shop. It was a linen shop. The dragon set fire to all the sheets and curtains. The shop assistants chased him out of the shop and down the road. He tried to hide in a doorway but set light to a very big mansion. The man who owned the mansion was very rich. He had a lot of dogs. They were angry because their kennels were burned. They joined in the chase. By now a large mob was chasing the dragon. He was very tired. The harder he ran the more he panted and the more fire he breathed. He hid in a copse in a beautiful park. That caught fire of course. The park-keepers joined in the chase waving pitchforks and rakes. He tried to hide behind an ice-cream van and melted all the ice-cream. The ice-cream man also joined in the chase. He blared out his chimes as loudly as they would go.

The dragon ran into the countryside. He found a huge pond. He said 'I must put out this fire in my throat.' He drank and drank but the fire still burned. The water started to get hot and to steam and to sizzle. The ducks quacked at him. They were afraid.

The dragon turned away and walked down a stony road. It was very cold. He came to some poor people living by the roadside. Their children were shivering and trying to sleep. Suddenly they woke up. What was this lovely warmth filling their hut? They went outside. The dragon was sitting in the road breathing fire. The poor people were very pleased to see him. They didn't chase him away and so he didn't bump into anything or hide inside anything and so he didn't set fire to anything. He toasted their sandwiches. And they named the dragon Summer because he brought them good times.

The people came from the city. It was a fortified city, by

the way. Round it there was a high grey wall. The gate was
made of iron spikes. They looked like rusty teeth. The people
from the city said the dragon was dangerous. He would set
fire to all the fields. The poor people said he wouldn't as long
as no one chased him into the fields. The people from the city
said the poor people were as dangerous as the dragon and they
would all be chased away. So the poor people sighed and set
Dragon Summer onto the people from the city and he burned
them all up.

The Boy Who Threw Bread on the Water

A young boy read in a big book 'Cast your bread upon the
waters and it shall be returned to you after many days.' So he
went to the Serpentine in Hyde Park. He threw his bread
upon the waters and sat down to wait. He knew he would
have to wait many days but he didn't know how many. This
meant he couldn't go away and come back. It might happen
that his bread would be returned while he was away and
someone else would get it. He waited three days. Then a
policeman came to arrest him for loitering with suspicious
intent. The boy said 'I'm waiting for my loaf.' The policeman
asked him where it would come from. The boy pointed to the
lake. The policeman arrested him. In court the magistrate
sent him to a madhouse to have his head examined.

A priest visited the boy in the madhouse. He bought the
boy a present. It was a copy of the same big book. The boy
said he thought the book was misleading. He said he had cast
his bread upon the waters but it had not been returned to
him. The priest explained to him that the book did not mean
what it said. It had to be interpreted. The boy said 'Who is to
interpret it?' The priest said 'The priests.' The boy said
'Well, what does the line about casting your bread on the

waters mean?' The priest said 'Well, there is much disagree-
ment about that.' The boy said – and you must remember
that he was very angry because he was sitting in a madhouse –
that god must be a great fool to have all that power and still
not be able to write clearly. The priest was shocked. He told
the magistrate the boy was wicked. The magistrate sent him
to prison.

I'm sorry to say the boy behaved badly in prison. The first
morning he was sentenced to solitary confinement. They
took him down to the punishment cells. They locked him in.
After a while the door opened. The warden handed him his
dinner. It was bread and water. He ate the bread and drank
the water. Here you see the wisdom of man contrasted with
the wisdom of god.

The Boy Who Tried to Reform the Thief

A boy was playing in the playground. A big boy came up to
him and stole his apple. Before the big boy had taken two
mouthfuls of the apple the little boy kicked him in the shins.
A master was looking from an upstairs window. He hurried
down to the playground. He grabbed the little boy by the
collar and pulled him away from the big boy. The little boy
said 'He stole my apple.' The teacher said 'I saw him steal it.
That was a very bad thing. But two wrongs don't make a
right. When someone injures us we must appeal to their
reason. We must explain that it's wrong to steal and then we
must ask for our property back. That is what civilized people
do.' The little boy said, 'But he wouldn't have given me my
apple. He'd have eaten it.' 'No doubt' said the teacher,
'nevertheless, where is your apple now? Look, it fell to the
ground and was trodden on in the fight. Now no one can eat
it. And your collar is torn and your face is bleeding. It is true

that by doing the right thing you would not have got your apple back. But then you wouldn't have been cut and your clothes wouldn't have been torn. And what is more: you would have had the satisfaction of doing right. For virtue is its own reward. And the reward of virtue is better than a pound of apples.' The teacher was very pleased. There was the crushed apple lying on the ground and it almost seemed as if it was agreeing with him.

Next day the boy was walking past the staff room. He looked in the window and saw the teacher tied to the chair and with a gag in his mouth. And there in a corner was a thief in front of the open safe. He was stealing the wages of the masters. The teacher was very pleased when he saw the boy peering in. When the boy disappeared from the window he sighed (secretly, because he didn't want the thief to hear) with relief. He said to himself 'The boy has gone to telephone the police. Soon I shall be rescued.' Imagine his surprise when the door opened and the boy walked in. The thief was also surprised. The boy carefully closed the door behind him. The boy knew that good boys do not leave doors open.

The teacher said to himself – he couldn't say it aloud because he was gagged – 'What a brave boy. He's come to tackle the thief single-handed. Soon I shall see him kick the thief in the shins. Of course it's very foolish of him to tackle the thief alone. But at least the thief will be disturbed and will run away without our wages.'

The boy said to the thief 'This is a school in which we are taught to do the right thing. It is wrong to steal. So I must ask you to put the money back. I assure you that the satisfaction you will receive from returning the money to its rightful owners will far outweigh the satisfaction you will get from spending it on ice-cream and racing cars,' which are the sort of things the boy imagined the thief would spend it on. The boy continued 'Of course I know that you may very well not return the money. In fact I'd be very surprised if you did.

Nevertheless my teacher is wiser than me and I must try to do what he would do in these circumstances. Fortunately he has already told me what that would be. And so I will say what he would have said if he were not gagged.' And while the thief carefully bundled up the ten pound notes and put them in his bag the boy told him of all the delights that are the reward of virtue. From time to time the master made gurgling noises behind the gag. The boy was pleased because the noises sounded very enthusiastic and he was glad to see how eagerly the master responded to the way he repeated his lesson. The thief said 'Thank you for talking to me young man. I'm glad to see that the standards of education are not slipping. It's obvious you're being taught all a gentleman should know. I must go now.' The boy said, 'Thank you for allowing me to address you.' The thief and the boy shook hands and just in time the boy remembered that it would be the polite thing to do to see the thief to the school gate. There he found a large car waiting and he opened and shut the door for the thief and waved goodbye as he drove away. He went back to the staff room. He cut the ropes tying the teacher to the chair. The teacher pulled the gag from his mouth. I regret to tell you – and we must understand that it is very uncomfortable to be tied up for an hour – that the teacher kicked the boy in the shins. Then he rushed out shouting 'Stop thief' and telephoned the police. Later the headmaster severely reprimanded the boy and he was almost expelled. He could not understand why.

When the teacher came home without his wages his wife was angry. She wouldn't talk to him for a week and fed him only on bread and butter for a month. He tried to explain to her the rewards she would receive from behaving in a civilized way. She wouldn't listen.

The Good Traveller

Hear the story of the good traveller and what followed from his great kindness.

A poor man lay at the roadside. He had been beaten up by soldiers. His head bled. He came to and reached a decision. The soldiers were hired by the Marquis. He lived in a great fortress. He sent out the soldiers to rob the countryside and cower the people. He didn't care what the soldiers did as long as they brought him back money and goods when they returned from their raids and as long as the people continued to bow to the ground when he was carried about in his palanquin. As the poor man came to he decided he had nothing left to live for. He would steal into the fortress and murder the Marquis. He knew he would not get out and that the soldiers would kill him. But at least he was sure he would get in. He was thin enough to get through a tiny crack in the wall. To seal his resolution he dashed his begging bowl to the ground. It broke into tiny pieces.

It was at this moment that the good traveller came along the road. He saw the poor man dash his begging bowl to pieces. He said to himself 'This man's despair is so great that he breaks his begging bowl that he might die more quickly.' It happened that the traveller was a merchant. It was the evening of market day. At the market he had cheated a silly old man by giving him a few coppers for a fine silver candlestick. He had told the silly old man that the silver candlestick wasn't worth much because it was only one of a pair. Next he took a table back from a young woman who had already paid half its price. Her husband had suddenly fallen ill. She asked for more time to pay what she owed. The merchant said it was against the rules of the Market Committee. This wasn't true but it made it seem to the young woman that nothing could be gained by arguing with him because she knew (so he thought) that he would not break the law. Instead the young woman cursed him. This upset him. He happened to have become more superstitious since he had started to pay the priests to pray for the security of the great chests in his cellars.

He took the table from her house and sold it to someone else. He had been troubled in mind ever since he left the market. When he saw the destitute man he said to himself, 'It would be as well to do a good deed and thus remove the curse.' He gave the man a coin. It was quite a large coin because the day's business had been good.

What starving man would not think of meat and bread and wine when he is suddenly given a large coin? The idea of killing the Marquis went completely out of his head. He ran to town and feasted and drank. Nor did he forget to take his wife and children to share his table at the tavern. And there was some money left over. The poor man said to his wife 'Think, wife. If I had gone off to kill the Marquis I would not have been at the roadside when the good traveller passed.' His wife said 'And I and our child would never have seen you again.' If the unaccustomed presence of food in her stomach had not made her so happy she would have cried. The poor man said 'I shall never lose patience again.'

Now god had watched all this from his window. He thought of all the other poor men who begged at the roadside. Then he thought of the silly old man who had been cheated and of the young woman who had lost her table. Her husband had just died so she had another reason to need comfort. God decided to send an angel to them all with a message of hope. The angel came down and whenever he saw the people suffering he told them the story of the good traveller. They were, he told them, to live in hope. It might happen that on any day someone would give them a large coin. Who could say? What's more, god had seen into the heart of the poor man. So the angel was able to tell them that the good traveller had even

saved him from committing the mortal crime of murder.
'Yes' said the angel 'but for this good deed the Marquis would
have been murdered that very night.'

When the poor people heard this they ran after the angel
and threw stones at him. The angel had to fly back to heaven
with some of his feathers missing.

The good traveller went smiling on his way and the cries of
the poor, the widowed and orphaned, the beaten and impris-
oned, rose to heaven. But god had turned away when he saw
how the wicked had stoned his ministering angel.

The Cheat

One day Billy sat his examinations. The questions were hard.
He couldn't answer all of them. He looked over his friend's
arm. He saw the answers neatly written down on his friend's
sheet of paper. He copied them onto his own sheet of paper.
The master saw him spying and copying. Billy didn't pass the
exam and what's more he was punished.

That night he was too upset to sleep. He went downstairs
for a glass of water. Passing the sitting-room door he heard
his father plotting with his mates to burn down the house on
the corner of the street. They didn't like the man who lived in
it. His skin was a different colour to Billy's and his Dad's.
Billy said to himself 'Spying again! Shall I tell my teacher
what I've heard? It would make the man who lives in the
corner house happy if I told my teacher. But I cheated at the
exam because I wanted to pass and make my father happy.
My father says he can't get a good job because he didn't pass
any exams. But if it's wrong to cheat to make even your father
happy it *must* be wrong to cheat to make the man in the corner
house happy. I will say nothing.' But he was very unhappy

when the corner house burned down. The man who lived in it was also burned. He had to go to hospital.

Now the man's son was Billy's classmate. They often played together. But Billy didn't enjoy their games anymore. He felt sad. He decided to ask the master about it. He went to him and said 'I knew my father was going to burn the house down. I didn't tell because that would be cheating. Now I don't like to play anymore.'

The master beat Billy. His Dad and his mates were sent to prison. And of course Billy's classmate wouldn't sit by him anymore. Everyone looked at Billy and said 'What d'you expect? Comes from a criminal background.'

In time Billy grew up. He went to work in a government office. He found lots of plans in a cabinet. One plan showed a town in the next country. It showed where his country was going to drop bombs on it. The plan said that the town and everything in it would be burnt to cinders. Billy thought back over his education. He decided to tell the people in the next country that they were going to be burned. He took the plan from the cabinet and put it in an envelope. He was seen posting the envelope by a suspicious superior. The superior was suspicious because he knew about Billy's criminal background. A special order was issued instructing the postman to open the postbox and hand the envelope to a high official. The high official read the address on the envelope and then opened it. The plan was inside. Billy was shot.

The Fly

There was a poor man who could not pay the rent for his house. The landlord said he must pay it the next day or be thrown out of it. The poor man was in despair. His neighbours were too poor to lend him money.

The poor man said, 'I will walk through the town. Perhaps I will find a coin in the street.' He couldn't think of a more likely way of getting money. He walked through the town but did not find a coin or a brooch or anything of value. The dogs had even run off with the bones.

He was returning home down a narrow street. He did not know the street very well. He looked up at the houses on either side. In the upper window of one sat a man. He was very like the poor man only he smiled. The poor man looked in at the open door. Inside he saw a clean table and three chairs. The table had been carefully laid with plates and knives and spoons. There was even a piece of carpet on the floor. A child played on it with some sticks and stones. In the hearth there was a small fire. The housewife cooked a meal in a black pot. The food smelt good.

The poor man called up to the man in the window.

'You are my age. As it happens you look like me. Our hair is the same colour. I too have a wife and child. We live in the same quarter of our town. I live in a house much like this in the same sort of street. But I have no money.'

The man in the window looked down at the poor man and listened carefully to him.

The poor man went on 'Tomorrow when I can't pay my rent the landlord will throw us out on the street. The winter in these parts is cold. Already the first snow has fallen. We cannot live through winter on the streets!'

A fly settled on the cheek of the man in the window. His face twitched. The poor man saw this and said to himself 'He is moved. Whether by anger or pity I cannot tell.'

The poor man called up.

'We have sold our furniture. We have sold our clothes except for a few rags we dare not sell. We must wear something for decency's sake. Would you have us run through the streets as naked as the dogs? For my work I have a knife, a hammer and a dowel. If I sold these I would not be able to work even if someone wished to hire me. My situation would be without hope. I would never again earn another penny. Have pity on me, townsman.'

The man in the window leaned forward. He wanted to hear all that the poor man said. The fly buzzed round his head. He whisked it away angrily with his hand.

The poor man's heart sank. But he went on.

'Perhaps one day your child will not be able to play on the carpet. The fire will not burn in your hearth. Your wife will have nothing to cook in the pot. Your house will not fill with the good smell of food. Misery may come to any man in these hard times. Perhaps you will have to seek for a friend among strangers.'

The man in the window craned forward to hear the poor man. The fly settled on his nose. He shook his head angrily to be rid of it.

When the poor man saw this he gave a cry of despair. He turned and ran away down the street.

The man in the window was troubled by the poor man's strange behaviour. Next morning he set out to find him. He asked for a poor man who looked like himself and was that day to be thrown out of his house by the landlord.

Someone soon pointed out the house he was seeking. He knocked at the door. It was opened by a child. He looked in to the room. He saw the poor man stretched on the floor. Beside him a woman sat quietly weeping. The man said, 'What is the matter?' The woman answered, 'Last night my husband came home late. In despair he gave me his work tools to sell. Then he killed himself.'

The Tree

When the gods got tired of men they sent an angel to cut down the tree of the world. This tree is called Yggrisil. When it is cut down the world will die.

The angel was pleased to be of service to the gods. He reached the world and began to walk through the town. Towards evening he felt tired. He saw an old woman watching him from her doorway. She said 'What are you doing?' The angel said 'I am looking for the tree of the world. The gods have sent me to cut it down.'

Now the old woman was ambitious. She said to the angel 'My son is a woodman. He will find the tree and cut it down.'

The angel said 'If your son is a woodman he will be able to cut down the tree more quickly than I can. The gods will be pleased. But the gods told me to bring a piece of the tree to them so that they could know the tree was down.'

The old woman said 'My son will bring a piece of the tree to heaven.'

The angel thanked her. The old woman woke her son early next morning and said to him 'Go quickly and cut down the tree of the world. And don't forget to bring me some of the wood.' She hoped for a great reward when she took it to heaven.

But the gods changed their mind and decided to let men live. When the angel came back and told them the tree was not yet cut down they were glad. They sent him back to the old woman to tell her the tree was not to be cut down.

The old woman was angry when she heard this. She said to herself 'The angel is lying. He wants to take the piece of tree to the gods and get the reward.' She said to the angel 'Hurry along that path. You will reach my son in time to stop him cutting down the tree.' The old woman sent him on the wrong path.

When the son reached Yggrisil he cut it down. He chopped off some of the tree. The old woman and her son took it to heaven. The gods saw what had been done and were angry. They said to them 'We will not take the wood. But men and women will carry it forever.' That is how death came to the world.

A Dream

(for David Dapra)

A boy walking on the shore saw a grey thread. It ran into the sea. He picked up the end and began to pull. There was a weight on the other end. All the same he managed to pull it fairly easily. After pulling for half an hour there was so much thread on the shore that he decided to roll it into a ball. Otherwise it would have become tangled. He pulled all day. In the evening he went home.

Next day he came back. There was the ball of thread with the end disappearing into the sea. He began to pull and wind. He did this day after day. One day he realized that the thread he was winding was the sea itself. This excited him because it made him ask what was on the end of the thread.

His eyes became skilful. He was able to see that the sea was a thread twisting and winding round itself. Sometimes as he wound the thread snagged. Then he had to tug. Sometimes whole seas or oceans turned over as he tugged on the thread to release it.

The ball became very big. Soon it took up a large part of the world. It was so heavy that the land on which it rested began to dip. Soon the world was shaped like a valley holding the ball of thread and what was left of the sea.

After a time the ball was so big that the sea was only a lake on a little flat shore. The boy worried that if the ball got much larger then one day there might be no more space to hold it left in the world. He went on winding and there was just enough space. One day the boy came to the end of the sea. Fixed to the end there was a hook and on the hook a fish.

The boy was silent when he saw the fish writhing on the dry shore. He picked it up and climbed to the top of the ball of thread. The ball was as big as the world had once been. He sat on top of the world and looked down at the fish. He began to cry. A salty pool formed round the fish and it began to swim. The boy smiled.

The Rotten Apple Tree

An apple tree grew in a garden. This tree bore rotten fruit. From the moment the blossoms withered and the tiny apples began to grow they were rotten. As they grew the rottenness grew with them. They were bruised and soft and had a rank smell. Patches of skin were brown or black and mildew and white fur grew on the patches. The crows loved this rotten fruit. They cawed and tore at it with their beaks. You would think that the man who owned the tree would have cut it down after first having had it examined to see what caused the fruit to rot and to find out how to prevent it infecting other trees. But it was not so. The people of the village heard of the tree and came to see it. Its fame spread. Soon people travelled to it from far away. At the crossroads signs were erected so that pilgrims should not lose their way. People prayed to the tree to punish their enemies and kill their rivals. They brought the sick to it: crippled children, old blind people and people who were carried in litters and had not taken one step on the earth since they were born in it. Stories began to be told. A blind woman who had touched the bark saw – though a school of thought held that she had touched a root where it stuck out of the ground. A barrier was built round the tree so that the soil in which it grew should not be trampled to dust or mud. Guardians were appointed to stop worshippers removing twigs and pieces of bark. Relics were cut from the tree but these were sold at high prices to potentates, rich merchants and the intendants of cathedrals. The king sent pieces of bark to his allies as a special pledge of fidelity. Near The Garden of The Tree that Bore Rotten Fruit there was an orchard of apple, plum and pear trees. These were cut down and burned and the place where they had stood cemented over and used as a car park. Hotels were built and trade prospered. The village grew into a town. Pictures and models of the sacred tree were sold in the shops, even in breadshops and greengrocers. Cuttings were taken from the tree and planted in special places where there were temples for worshippers and houses in which the keepers of the trees could live. This transplanting was carefully regulated. It was done so well that in a few years many places boasted their own Rotten Fruit Trees. Indeed one city boasted of a small orchard of such trees. This caused consternation in the town where the first tree had grown. But its owner was a wise man and he told his fellow townsmen they had nothing to fear. The more Rotten Fruit Trees there were the more the mind of the nation would be turned on Rotten Fruit Trees. And the more the mind of the nation was turned on Rotten Fruit Trees the more they would venerate The First Rotten Fruit Tree. Even when it died and was replaced by one of its saplings people would still venerate the spot where it had grown. His fellow townsmen saw the sense of this – especially as he added that there were, after all, enough people to go round. People began to be ashamed of apple trees on which good fruit grew. Wives complained to their husbands about them. Schoolboys threw stones at the windows of houses that stood in gardens where they grew. Crowds of drunken youths swung on their branches to break them. Residents Associations sent letters to those who grew and protected them. All over the country you could hear the sound of the axe. When the people had cut down the good apple trees they cut down the good pear trees, good plum trees and good cherry trees. They tore up the raspberry canes and gooseberry bushes. No one wished to be accused of protecting any tree, bush or shrub that could be regarded as an insult to The Great Bearer of Rotten Apples and all The Lesser Bearers of Rotten Apples that had been grown from it. The day was made dark and the night was made bright by the fires which consumed them. Action Groups of Tree Fellers were trained in the expert use of axe and saw and hauling chain. They began to chop up furniture. First they chopped up furniture made of apple wood. Then because it could be difficult to tell the tree from which the wood had come they chopped up all wooden furniture. Next they chopped up wooden doors, wooden picture frames, wooden fences and every other wooden thing – except for Rotten Apple Trees and their Relics. A faker was arrested for sticking rotten chestnuts on a tree and claiming it to be the first Rotten Nut Tree. After a spectacular trial – during which many women fainted and one woman threw a box of sawdust in the faker's eyes – and which the judge summed up in a voice that quivered as he described the danger in which he saw youth standing – the faker was condemned and shot by bow and arrow on National Rotten Apple Day before a great crowd of people who as a sign of contempt for his heresy had stained their faces, hands, clothes and shoes with the pulp of rotten apples. They ended the day by dancing round a giant effigy of William Tell's Son with a replica of the historic rotten apple on his head – the fact that it was a rotten apple had been established by the researches of the country's leading university. Music for the dancing was provided by a chorus of children dressed as apple leaves. The country is now in a state of high readiness.

The people are dedicated to the worship of Old Pippin – as The First Rotten Apple Tree has now declared itself (through The Senior Oracle) to be named. All Old Pippin's enemies dwell in fear. They are said to shake like aspen leaves. The government has declared it an article of religion and a fact of science that neither the leaves nor the branches of Rotten Apple Trees shake. The arts of chopping with the axe and cutting with the saw are zealously taught in schools and Felling Institutions. Workers are required to practise felling for the nation for one hour a day after the end of their normal work. It is true that the nation has run out of trees – except for rotten apple trees which of course may not be touched. It has even run out of wood – since the coffins were removed from churchyards in the Special Night Actions. So there is nothing left to fell. But as the Leader of the Action Groups said to a mass rally of Fellers drawn from all parts of the country and with contingents from abroad 'We are loyal, devoted, trained and eager for whatever our task may be. We stand ready with axe in hand. We merely await the order of our Leader.'

The Call

A woman heard a voice calling from time to time in the mountains. She would take a short walk into the foothills to see if she could find who it was that called. Sometimes she was away whole days. But she did not find who called. She could not even be sure where the calls came from. There were so many rocks and slopes and paths. The calls seemed to come along the paths. But to make it worse sometimes the rocks seemed to be calling. Perhaps this was the echo. Soon the woman listened for the call all the time. She would wake up and lie in bed or go out in the yard and every hour or so hear quite clearly single shouts coming from the mountain. At last she decided she would find out who made them. She packed a few things and went into the mountains. When she had eaten her provisions she ate wild food. There was plenty of clear water in the streams. On the lower slopes there were isolated farms. She would go to the wooden farm houses and ask for food. In return she was asked to do a little work. Higher up she met a few goatherds. They gave her milk. When she asked about the calls they shrugged their shoulders. They had heard them for so many years that now they ignored them. Only at first had they set out to search for someone trapped in the mountains. Now they were certain it was the sound of the wind or falling rocks amplified by the passes. The woman thought they were afraid of the calls and went into their hut and shut the door on the days when the voice called all the time. The woman went higher, following the paths down which the calls came. One day she sat on a rock and said 'My life is now a bundle of sticks tied with a string. I have given up everything to find the voice.' So she went on. Sometimes on the higher ranges the sun shone brightly but often there was a snow-storm or a silent mist that stretched for miles. At such times she rested in a crevice. She was nearer the voice. Away from all other noises except those of the wind, springs and rocks, the calls were very clear. She called to it but there was no answer: there was only every hour or so the same brief, sharp call. She followed the voice to the highest peak. She stood on it and was confused. No one else was there. Then she looked round and because it was the highest peak she could see the whole world. There was a shout of protest at what she saw. She realized that the shout came from her own mouth and that it had always been her voice she had heard on the mountain. She went down the mountain. It was easier than climbing up. She did not go to her village. She went on new travels. At first wherever she went she cried with the short sharp calls she had heard. Later she learned to talk to people. But the sound of the mountain calls never left her voice. She told those who still mocked her that they had not seen the world.

On the Pride of Some Who Rule

A ruler sailed back from war to his country. By accident he dropped his golden ring into the sea. This made him sad at his homecoming.

A month later fishermen caught a large fish. They took it to the palace and it was cooked for the king. When it was cut open before him there in the stomach was the golden ring.

The king said 'See how the gods favour me!' This pleased him and he was very proud.

When he was a little older he needed to show the people that the gods still loved him. He went to the quay and threw his ring over the sea. A seagull flying in to land saw it glittering as it fell. It snatched it out of the air and flew with it towards the quay. When it found that the thing in its mouth was as hard as stone it dropped it. It landed on the quay at the king's feet. His courtiers marvelled.

The king boasted of his good standing with the gods. To prove it he often threw away his ring. Into crowded streets, dark forests, thickets, swamps, battlefields – it was always returned to him and his courtiers marvelled.

One day he saw a man ploughing a field. He shut his eyes and threw his ring into the field. But the ploughman couldn't plough it up: the ring was lost. The king had the ploughman disposed of and went home. He was not worried. He said 'The ring will be returned to me. I am a favourite of the gods.'

A year later the king was hunting. The huntsmen chased a deer through the forest. It escaped and vanished into the deepest part of the forest where the trees were thickest. The king chased it for a while and then stopped. He wasn't sad. His forests were full of game. He decided to step down from his horse and rest. A wild boar stepped out onto the path. The huntsmen blew their horns. The boar charged and caught the king just as he stepped down from his horse. It gored him fatally in the stomach. On the tusk of the boar that killed him the courtiers found the golden ring.

The Cliffs

The cliffs were proud of their height. They strained to hold their heads even higher. Because of this they could not see clearly what happened at their feet. But they were proud of the constant fawning of the sea. Often the sea would try to run away from them but it would never go far. Always it returned to the foot of the cliffs often more boisterous and fervent than before but sometimes quietened and humbled. The cliffs were stoic and brave as they faced the sky. They regarded with contempt – or compassion – the listless turmoil of the sea, so unstable, so inconstant. And at first they did not know what was happening when one day, their foundations having been burrowed into and eaten out, they fell down into the sea and it washed them away.

Not a Tragedy but an Error, Not an Absurdity but a Mistake

A man may be struck dumb on the day he has learned a new language. But there are those people who are absurd and tragic in their own behaviour. It's wrong to criticize the world as if it resembled such people. I have in mind those, for example, who climb for the highest apple in the tree. They pick it and carelessly drop it as they look for a higher apple. Then they complain that they have lost the highest apple. Some of them have become so much creatures of habit that they even try to climb into the sky. They reach out on the slender branches and of course they over-reach themselves and fall through the tree. We find them lying dead in the grass beside the apple they had picked and dropped. But it would be ridiculous to call the *tree* tragic or absurd.

A Man Sat on a Gate

A man sat on a gate to watch the world go by. He sat there so long and grew so fat that the gate fell off its hinges. The man toppled over backwards and lay on the ground with his mouth open. From then on he lay there. No doubt he studied the great engine of the universe as it displayed itself to him in the sky but as he was unable to move his mouth to speak or his hands to write (the fall had paralysed him) he was unable to tell us. Eventually a bird nested in his open mouth. It would be pleasant to say that the birds who were hatched and reared so close to what might well have been the fountain of truth had the secrets of the engine whispered to them and carried it aloft on their wings. But it would never be true to say this.

The Wise Man Who Broke His Vow

A man vowed as a protest against the war of the rich on the poor that he would not open his eyes till the people had won justice. Many things happened that might have made him open his eyes in surprise. A car crashed. A door shut on his hand. A wasp stung him. A dog bit his leg. People shouted at him for being a fool. His wife and children pleaded with him. His dying mother asked him to look at her. Then there was the weariness of walking the streets like a blind man. Many of the things that had once been easy to do now became labours. In all this he kept his eyes closed.

One day as he passed an open doorway he heard a mother on the doorstep saying farewell to her son as he stepped into the street. The man learned from their farewell that the son was a poorman going to fight for the rich against the poor. His mother told him he must obey his officers like a good boy and be brave. The man who had vowed to shut his eyes said 'The sight of some things is more terrible than blindness. And I must look at them.' He opened his eyes and watched the soldier in his smart uniform, with the buttons shining as brightly as his eyes, as he smartly marched away down the street to fight for the rich against the poor. The man said 'I was a fool to shut my eyes. I must see these things so that I will never stop fighting for the poor against the rich.'

Water

In a certain city there had been for many hundreds of years a shortage of water. This caused disease and other suffering to the citizens. Each spring there was a heavy rainfall and the silent people watched the precious life-stream running in gutters that would soon be as dry as bone. In time modern machines were constructed. There were new spinning factories and iron foundries in the city. These places needed more water and so did the new workers. The city's rulers were practical and philanthropic men. They used their new machines to build a dam in the hills over the city. The dam collected all the water the city needed. Unfortunately, when the spring rains fell, the lake behind the dam became too full. There was a danger that the pressure of water would explode and engulf the city in sudden destruction. The dam wall shook like the hand of a sick man. This terrified the workers and some of them ran away from the factories and lived in the hills. In the general panic there was rioting and looting. Priests held special services. Factory owners called on the government to enforce law and order.

As the rulers of the city had been clever enough to build the dam they ought to have been clever enough to make it safe. They might have built aqueducts to take the water safely round the city or through the parks and squares to make them beautiful with lakes and fountains. But understand that there was panic and fear of collapse. In such times rulers don't blame the machinery of society but its people. Indeed they look on disaster as a test of national spirit. So instead of reconstructing the dam the rulers called on the citizens to serve their city with greater efforts: they were to drink more water.

Water drinking festivals were organized. Drinking squads patrolled the streets. The good citizen was seen at all times sipping from a glass of water in his hand. Medals were given to those who consumed large quantities. It's surprising what well-intentioned and public-spirited individuals can do on such occasions. One man drank fifty gallons of water each week for three weeks running before he drowned internally. He asked to be buried in a bath. There was much washing of the person and of possessions. People whose curtains were not constantly dripping could expect to have their windows broken by groups of young pioneers who were called The Water Babies. As the whole city was damp and as people went about in clothes that had been laundered to shreds and slept in damp beds, there was a lot of influenza about. Newspapers published daily casualty lists. These showed great increases in the number of cases of pneumonia. People also suffered from water on the knee and on the brain. Because the door-steps and streets were washed so often, many people slipped and the casualty service had to deal with sprained ankles and broken legs and backs. Of course the wounded – who had already made the sacrifice – could no longer drink very much or wash very often. The burden fell more heavily on the rest.

About this time patriotic people began to set fire to their houses so that firemen could hose them down. Loyalists also burned public buildings such as galleries, museums and schools. Nothing could be allowed to impede the city's efforts. National security was at stake. We can confidently say that the people's morale was never higher. And it worked. The level of water behind the dam fell. This overwhelming argument was used against those few disruptive elements who asked whether there might not be an easier way of controlling the dam. The dam wall no longer trembled. Dissenters were taken to their cell windows and made to stare up at it and declare that it stood as firm as a rock. Every day the media reminded the people of the days when the dam had been called Old Palsied and they had lived in fear of The Burst. Things were going well. All the more reason, then, for the massive outbreak of dropsy to come as such a severe blow to the regime. This blow was followed by another: people began to burst. The rulers even wondered if the people could hold out. As the governor looked from his window he saw passers by fall over in the streets and roll to the side of houses and lie there for minutes at a time without drinking. Perhaps there were inherent weaknesses in the national character. How could such a nation survive?

The Governor himself felt worn out by the struggle against water. He decided to address the people – perhaps, he told himself, for the last time. The Water Police rounded up the survivors and assembled them on the main square. The governor was surprised at the smallness of the crowd. If the people had not been so bloated he would have seen that it was even smaller than he thought. As the governor spoke one or two exploded. A new illness had broken out: a fever which heated the blood and so caused the water to boil. Sufferers emitted large amounts of steam and a high whistling scream from their ears, mouth, nose and anus till their bodies burst. The governor spoke with great dignity, raising his voice over the screaming, blurping, plopping, pissing and exploding. 'Fellow citizens! This morning the figures were delivered to my desk. The level of water in the dam is now so low that – should any of you survive – you will be assured of three whole years without danger of a dam burst. What the future holds beyond then we cannot tell, but these three years are safe – no matter how much rain falls! Citizens I salute your great victory! God bless us!' He then became over-heated with patriotic fervour and began to boil. He screamed and emitted a cloud of steam. The crowd had counted up to five before he exploded. As spring rainclouds gathered on the hills water police went among the crowd using the new-fangled hose-and-pump contraptions that had recently been introduced to enable them to pump water down the gullet of those who, however willing, were unable to swallow any more.

There was a Cunning Wealthy Man

There was a cunning wealthy man who coveted a poorman's house. The poorman did not wish to sell it. It was where he and his wife and children lived. They would have great trouble in finding another house. But the cunning rich man was determined to get the house. He did not wish to give money for it. Instead he waylaid the man. He did this himself because although he was wealthy he did not like to pay others to do work he could do himself. One evening he waited in a shop doorway. He stepped out as the man passed and killed him with a cudgel. He left his body in the street. The dead man's wife saw this. She had been watching in a window of the house for his return. Her neighbours pitied her but they would do nothing against the murderer. He was too powerful. He sent his bullies round to the house and they chased the woman and her children into the street. He had to pay the woman a little money or his title to the house would not have been legal. But he paid her less than he would have paid her husband because he said her story that he had killed him had given him a bad name.

Now the rich man wished to take up public office. His friends in the government were worried. They wished all officials to appear as men of honour. The woman's stories had blackened him. The cunning man said he would stand trial so that his name might be cleared. Then he would become the government's good servant. He was to be in charge of social services. So his friends charged him with the poorman's murder. He briefed a great lawyer who was as cunning and powerful as himself. In the meantime he heard that the poorman's widow had died of misery and exposure or something. This made the case against him even weaker. Now all the evidence would be hearsay. It is true that the dead man's children were also witnesses of the crime. They had been waiting in the doorway of their house for their father's return. But as yet they had not learned to speak and could only cry when they saw the cunning man. And so the lawyer went into court with his fat brief under one arm and his cunning friend's arm under the other. And then happened one of those things that our experience of life does not lead us to expect. As the cunning man entered the court he looked up. There in the judge's chair for all to see was the ghost of the dead woman – pointing her finger at him.

Now this story is not true. People do not come back from the dead armed with a power to do those things they did not do, either from weakness or neglect, when they were alive. If justice was to be done to the memory of the dead man and woman, and the house restored to their children, this would have to be done by the neighbours.

Incident on the Island of Aigge

A fisherman on the island of Aigge was caught carrying the carcass of a sheep which was the property of the Laird of Aigge. He was hanged for sheep stealing. His body was left on a gibbet by the shore. As he was hanged on the afternoon of the day he was caught his wife did not know he had been hanged when a message reached her telling her to collect his body for burial.

The woman had a child of seven months. She had no neighbour to mind it and so she took it with her in the boat when she went to collect her husband's body. When she was three-quarters of the way across the bay she could see the body hanging on the gibbet on the shore. The child slept, nursed by the rocking of the boat.

She beached the boat and with his fisherman's knife she cut down her husband from the gibbet. There was no one on the beach to help her and so she partly lifted and partly hauled the body to the boat. Its feet dragged on the shingles.

She lay the body on the bottom of the boat and as there was little room she lay the child on its father's breast. The child felt the human body and mistook the rocking of the boat for being rocked in its arms and so it reached out to embrace it. It happened that the child's warmth warmed the man's throat and chest. It was this and perhaps also the rocking of the boat that stirred a glimmering of life in the man. The hardships he had lived through had made him strong and even on the rope he had clutched to himself a last draining of life. The woman saw the man's hand move on the child's back. She rested the oars on the bottom of the boat and chafed and rubbed his body. Soon she heard his faint breathing. When she got home she wrapped him in a blanket by the fire and in a few days he had recovered. In this way the child gave life to its father even before it could speak its father's name.

The Letter

One day just before she went to bed a woman looked through her bedroom window at the sky. It was covered with mist. There was a full moon and a patch of moonlight shone through the mist. It reminded the woman of the circle of churning water left by someone who had thrown themself from a bridge. Immediately she thought of her daughter. She had married and gone with her husband to live in a distant town. The woman said 'I have not heard from her for months. I would like to know how she is. Tomorrow I will write to her.' The next day the woman was busy. She worked in a factory and cooked for her husband and ran their home. So she did not write.

The day after she was shopping and saw in a shop window the naked body of a dummy lying on the floor. Its arms were awkwardly bent. A man knelt beside it. Immediately the woman thought of her daughter and wondered how she was. She said 'I will write to her this evening.' That evening she did the washing and ironing.

The next day the woman heard that fifty of the newer girls at the factory were to be sacked. She saw one of them leaving the factory. She carried an empty shopping bag and her face was white. She had lately moved into a new house. She and her husband had both worked and so had been able to afford the mortgage repayments. Again the woman thought of her daughter. She said 'I wonder how she manages in these hard

times? Tomorrow is Saturday and I will write.' On Saturday
the woman finished her weekly cleaning before lunch. After
lunch she sat down for a short rest. She said 'Have I told her
her cousin has had a baby? I must think what to write to her.
She'll be as worried about me as I am about her. I must
reassure her. Perhaps there'll be no more sackings at the
factory . . .' The woman was tired and dozed till her husband
came in and woke her. She cooked their supper and after that
there was no time to write.

On Sunday she felt rested. She cleared a space on the
corner of the kitchen table. She looked in the shoe box where
she kept a writing pad and envelopes. It was empty. She went
next door to her neighbour Mrs Harrison to borrow some
paper and an envelope but Mrs Harrison didn't have any.

Fortunately when the woman got home from work on
Monday there was a letter from her daughter on the doormat.
She made herself a cup of tea and sat at the table to read the
letter. Her daughter was well and getting on with her husband. Both of them had work. She was friendly with her
neighbours. The weather in the North was colder than at
home but she was getting used to it.

The woman's tea was stronger than the canteen tea and she
enjoyed it. She picked up the newspaper and began to read. A
fly settled on a photograph of an African family massacred in
their village.

Service

A Story

The form came in the morning post. It was printed on better paper than most forms. There was also a brochure explaining the duties of jurors and their role in the administration of the law. Part of the form was to be sent back. He was asked to state on this part his willingness to serve or his reasons for asking to be excused. He didn't think very seriously about it. He wrote down his reasons for asking to be excused and sent the form back.

A week later another form came. It said the official who sent the forms couldn't accept his reasons and he would have to serve. But the form said there was an automatic reconsideration of the official's decision. This was made by a judge in chambers. He could attend and explain his reasons to the judge. But he did not have to attend. If he did not attend the judge would make his decision on the reasons written on the form. He decided to attend.

The new form said he should report to the court at 10.15. He got there on time. There were a few policemen in the corridor outside and two women reading a notice pinned to the wall by the court door. He looked through the glass panel of the court door. He could see along one side of the court. It was empty. It reminded him of a glass aquarium. He went out into the street and looked in the window of a record shop. One of the covers showed a pistol being fired straight at the spectator.

He went back. He was going to ask the policeman at the door where he should go but he didn't. His name wasn't on the list of names on the notice pinned by the door. He didn't know the other names. About thirty people were there now. A young man leaned against a wall. He was wearing a brown wool shirt and blue jeans. He had a small empty push-pram in front of him. The hood and sides were bright blue. He was holding the rail with both hands. He looked at the man and noticed with quiet shock that the man was afraid. There were a few women on a bench. They were wearing best clothes and they'd done special things with their hair and this made them look rather ugly. They were silent. A man with well creased trousers was reading a *Daily Express*. There were two male ushers in black gowns. They were old, retired men making a little pocket money. They chatted in a quiet relaxed way like discreet porters in a Pall Mall Club. There was also a woman usher for the children's court. She was middle-aged and had blond hair and a nice efficient face. A door opened and some barristers shot out and swept towards him. Most of them were young. He supposed the older barristers usually went to bigger courts. They wore black gowns and little wigs tightly curled like the hair of the woman on the bench. The wigs were grey and this made the young men look strange. They didn't look at the people waiting in the corridor. Perhaps they were going to see clients in the cells. The young man with the pram still leaned against the wall and he looked up as the lawyers passed. One of the women tugged at her skirt to smooth it.

Suddenly he walked out. He strolled round the market in front of the court. It was sunny. He stayed there ten minutes. Then he went home.

A few days later a registered letter came. He was summoned to explain why he had failed to attend as a juror. 10.15 in a week's time. Penalty £100.

So in a week's time he went back. He didn't bother to get there till 10.30. There were about ten people waiting. He recognized some of them. They'd been there on his first visit. That had been on the opening day of the new sessions. Now even the ordinary citizens seemed a bit more at home. They had learned some nonchalance. Perhaps from imitating the lawyers. But their little smiles seemed awkward and their relaxed poses still slightly uncomfortable. The glossy smiles of people in hospital. He felt more at home too. He began making little jokes to himself. Chin up, as the hangman said to the victim.

A dark figure came into the light at the end of the corridor. A tall man in a dark blue suit. The face was hidden against the light but it was obviously round. He carried a heavy briefcase and in the other hand a lumpily rolled umbrella. He held the umbrella up in the air so that the ferrule was about eighteen inches off the ground. But the odder thing was his hat. It was an old-fashioned hat. A bit like a pork-pie but formal and dark. He hadn't seen a hat like that before. The man nodded to the policeman and went through a small door that obviously led to the back of the court. There was an air of caricature about the man – and he knew immediately it was the judge. He didn't like that. He didn't like people to look their role so exactly that they seemed to be imitating themselves.

He asked the usher where he should go. The usher already knew about him and had been told his name. The usher was very polite. He said the jury in waiting would soon be called into court and he was to go in with them and sit on the bench in front of them.

During the week he'd phoned an organization concerned with civil liberties. They'd said there was no modern precedent. But if he served he could return whatever verdict he liked. Even a verdict against the evidence. Even though you had to take the juror's oath? There was a precedent for it. The seventeenth century. Penn and another Quaker. A jury had refused to convict them for refusing to serve on a jury. A judge had locked the jury up without bread or water. But they still refused to convict . . . It wasn't only a matter of £100. That was for refusing to answer the summons to appear. If he now appeared and still refused to serve that would be contempt of court. Prison. Till you apologized. Or agreed to serve? And a friend explained to him that if you said it was your busy time at work or your grandmother was dying, they'd always excuse you. But if you objected on principle, that was a challenge. And the judge wouldn't ignore that. Dying grandmother – the juror's Chiltern Hundreds. He was making these jokes to himself because he was nervous.

The usher said 'Let's go' and the jury hurried into court. The space between the side of the dock and the benches was small so they had to walk in single file. He walked at the end. He hadn't walked in single file since he was in the army. The judge came in. Everyone stood up. The judge wore a grey robe with red and blue sashes crossed on his chest. He had a small grey wig. He was plumpish and his round face was red. The man hated all these details. It seemed so threatening, almost malicious, to appear so true to type.

The judge, the lawyers, and some of the jurymen bowed to each other. Then they all sat down. Suddenly a door opened somewhere at the back behind the dock. Two policewomen came out. They wore navy blue skirts, pale blue shirts with metal buttons and badges, and smart white and navy blue bonnets. Two healthy-looking blondes. With them they had a thin woman with a bony face and dark eyes, narrow little shoulders and bony hands. About fifty. She was wearing a dark blue overall-dress with thin red piping round all the edges. It was quite smart and fitted fairly well. It might have been designed by an airline for the cleaning women to wear when they cleaned the empty planes between flights. He didn't realize before she went into the dock and stood between the two policewoman that she was the accused.

The clerk told him to stand. The judge looked up from his papers. The judge smiled at him and asked why he had failed to attend as a juror. His voice was puzzled and kind. As if he was talking to a child who'd trod on his toe.

The man took the forms from his pocket. He was surprised

to see that his hand shook. He leaned against the side of the
dock to steady himself. He explained that he had been told he
could attend a hearing of an appeal against the official's
refusal to excuse him service. (He didn't say he had attended
but had gone away – in despair at seeing the frightened man
with the empty pram and the lonely women on the bench.)
He read the details from the form. The judge started to hunt
in his file for his copy. His voice trailed away and he waited
for the judge's attention. He said 'If I could go on . . . ?' He
was surprised to hear himself using this lawyer's phrase. The
judge went on searching and the silence lasted. The judge
found the form and looked up. Still shaking, he read out the
new summons about the £100 and about failing to attend
when summoned and said 'But I don't think I was summoned. The second summons was incorrect. I hadn't been
summoned to appear as a juror – only to hear the appeal. And
the form said I needn't attend if I didn't want to.' There was a
silence. Of course all these details weren't important. They
had nothing to do with his reason for refusing to serve. But he
was indignant that a false summons could be issued so easily.
Where was truth if even in little things it– ? The judge said, 'I
see you were under a misunderstanding about this summons
and I will take no further action on it' – he smiled kindly –
'but there is still the matter of your refusal to serve as a juror.
I've read the reasons you give on the acknowledgement form
and I must tell you I cannot excuse you on those grounds.'
The judge smiled again.

No, he thought. He still doesn't say it right. I was not
under a misunderstanding about the second summons. *He*
was. It was falsely issued. He was indignant that even this
small truth couldn't be seen and respected. He looked across
at the woman in the dock. Her eyes with the little dark pupils
were staring straight ahead at the judge. She had been
brought up from the cells and made to stand and listen to all
this. Was she relieved to have her case put off for ten

minutes? Or angry at being made to stand there while he talked about the first summons and the second summons and the appeal and the reasons?

A group of schoolchildren were packed into one box. They were there as part of their civic studies. To see how the court worked and how everyone had a chance to speak.

The judge smiled gently and said, 'Would you like to add anything to the reasons you state on the form?'

He was confused. He wasn't prepared. The form said he would be heard by a judge in chambers. But they were in open court. And he couldn't understand why he was so agitated. What more could he say? The reasons given on the form were perfectly adequate. They were enough for him. Why not for the judge? He said. 'No – just the moral and political reasons I put on the form.'

The judge was speaking again. 'Many people of different political persuasions . . . differing moral outlooks serve on the . . . Perhaps the last civic duty the citizens of this country are still called upon to . . . Freedom of our courts . . . The protection of the interests of the accused . . .'

He looked at the schoolchildren crammed in the box. Everyone here had public, court expressions. How could he tell what they were thinking? They might have been staring at a film he couldn't see.

In another box on their own were a girl and a young man. In Sunday best. Hair groomed. Staring at him and then at the woman in the dock. He knew immediately they were her children. Fair hair and blue eyes – and she was dark with tiny black pupils. But there must still be some family likeness he could sense. There was no man there. Perhaps she was a widow.

'. . . so that perhaps you were unaware that you are not required to decide on legal or moral matters but purely on questions of fact –'.

'But I dealt with that in the reasons I put on the form. I said

I couldn't agree with you what facts would be relevant. You want the record of a crime to begin at the time when the criminal thought of it. I want to know more. I said – there on the form – that when you desocialize people in schools – when you take away their responsibility in their work – how can you be surprised when they act anti-socially . . . ?'

The small court seemed to get larger. He could breathe in it. And although it seemed larger he didn't feel so lost. The judge and he started to argue.

Suddenly he remembered what had been in the back of his mind since he read the first form weeks ago. Two furniture vans were being driven across Germany. The windows had been sealed up and the sides reinforced. They had been requisitioned by the SS. They were driven through busy little towns and along open country roads all day till it was dark. Then they'd been parked in front of a row of little houses out in the open. The houses were separated from the road by a wide grass verge. The houses were dark because of the war. The lorry drivers had a smoke and stretched themselves across their seats to sleep. In the night the Jews in the vans had started to scratch and beat on the sides. They called for water, not even for something to eat. No light came on in the row of houses, no door opened, no curtain was pulled aside. The Jews were too weak and afraid to make much noise. The lorry drivers didn't even bother to shout at them – the vans were sealed anyway so the lorry drivers couldn't have carried out any threats even if they'd made them except perhaps to jolt them and give them a rough ride the next day. And the grass verge between the vans and the houses was wide. But still, the people in the houses had heard the Jews. In the morning the lorry drivers smoked a cigarette, started their lorries and drove to the crematorium.

It wasn't a good argument with the judge. Saint Joan would have done better. It ended in a silly way. The judge said unsmilingly 'You will serve,' and he said 'I will not'. The judge looked away and began to count to ten. He waited like a sheep until the judge had got to three before he said 'So what are you going to do about it?'

From time to time during the argument the lawyers sitting below the judge's bench had slowly turned round to look at him. Now they all stared at the judge.

The judge said 'I strongly advise you to sit down and wait to see if your name is called. Then, should they so wish it will be open to either the prosecution or the defence to object to your being on the jury. Either side may object to seven jurors without even giving a reason for doing so.'

For a moment he was puzzled. Was it a game?

The judge said, 'Perhaps your name won't even be called.'

He said angrily 'I hope not!' He sat down. He was still bewildered. He was unsure of what was happening.

The clerk of the court stood up. He took an envelope from the desk. He took a slip of paper from it and read out the name on it. A juror in waiting stood up, crossed the court, and went into the witness box. He'd seen him several times in the streets. He was a van driver for the town's biggest multiple store – a friendly-looking man who wore good jackets and ties because he got them on discount. The clerk took another slip from the envelope.

When his name was called he would go quietly into the jury box. The judge would pretend that nothing unusual had happened but he would grunt to himself with satisfaction that the force of the law had been upheld. Or probably he would sigh and smile with genuine contentment that the difficult juror had finally been sensible – as most people were in the end. But when the Bible was put into his hand for the oath he would ask the judge 'What book is this?'

The judge: 'The Bible'.

'Unlike my fellow jurors I haven't read it. Or even held it in my hand recently till now. I am perfectly prepared to swear on it. But I must read it first.'

The judge: 'How long will you need?

'It's a thick book on very thin paper and I see that it starts with the words "In the beginning God created the heaven and earth". It's obviously going to be a long story and I shall need at least two years.' And he would refuse to affirm instead of swearing because that would mark him off from the other jurors and put him at a disadvantage in their discussions. The judge would then threaten him with contempt of court and he would say 'If I were a judge, I would regard only one thing as contempt of my court: when someone didn't tell the truth in it. I have told the truth.' That would have done for Saint Joan.

The clerk put his hand into the envelope for the twelfth paper. Their eyes met. The judge was busy with his files. His name wasn't on it.

And so there was to be no confrontation. Instead the argument about truth had been disposed of by a game of administrative tiddly-winks. It seemed to have little to do with the dignity of the law. Just a piece of thieves' cunning. He sat on the bench and felt as crumpled as an empty sweet bag. Had his name even been in the envelope? It was so easy to avoid an unprofitable complication by a little official dexterity.

Each juror took the Bible and swore the oath. He'd expected starched collars but some of them were in shirt sleeves and without ties. A friend at work had said that he would have sat on the jury and refused to convict. But that had now been taken care of by more tiddly-winks: majority verdicts.

Everyone listened while the indictment and charges were read. The charges repeated the indictment but added more details. There were twenty-one charges. The woman answered not guilty to all of them. She was an accountant accused of taking her employers' money.

The judge dismissed the jurors who hadn't been called. He

apologized to them. He explained that it would be undemo-
cratic to call only the exact number of jurors needed. It was a
small town and some of them might have known the accused.
The judge smiled when he said that of course he understood
some of them were naturally disappointed at not being able to
have a go . . .

He was surprised at the judge's words. He might have used
an expression that didn't suggest the fun fair.